AN INTRODUCTION TO 20TH-CENTURY ARCHITECTURE

AN INTRODUCTION TO
20TH-CENTURY
ARCHITECTURE

LUCY PEEL ▪ POLLY POWELL ▪ ALEXANDER GARRETT

THE APPLE PRESS

A QUINTET BOOK

Published by The Apple Press
6 Blundell Street
London, N7 9BH

ISBN 1-85076-182-5

This book was designed and produced by
Quintet Publishing Limited
6 Blundell Street
London N7 9BH

Creative Director: Peter Bridgewater
Art Director: Ian Hunt
Designer: Jonathan Roberts
Project Editor: Judith Simons
Editor: James Clark
Picture Researcher: Liz Eddison

Typeset in Great Britain by
Central Southern Typesetters, Eastbourne
Manufactured in Hong Kong by
Regent Publishing Services Limited
Printed in Hong Kong by
Leefung-Asco Printers Limited

CONTENTS

GENERAL INTRODUCTION

How will the 20th century be judged by the future historians of architecture? To some extent, that question is inextricably tied to the destiny of human civilization.

For example, is it possible to imagine that a future century could spawn such a dramatic pace of technological change as has produced first the wireless telegraph and then the super-computer? If not, then how could architecture again stride the distance between the Carson, Pirie and Scott department store and the Hongkong & Shanghai Bank in the space of 100 years?

Indeed, set against an age that has seen the splitting of the atom and men landing on the moon, the speed at which architecture has changed this century may seem less impressive.

However, it will be difficult for future chroniclers of architectural history to conclude that the 20th century has been anything less than revolutionary. It is a time when architecture has become truly international for the first time, when local influences have been subordinated to a global style, and when the traditions of East and West have converged.

The buildings of today are constructed using many materials that had not been invented a 100 years ago, and the role of the craftsman in their creation has been largely superseded by factory mass-production. And the architects of this century have found new masters. No longer the exclusive servants of governments and wealthy patrons, architects have found themselves as often designing factories and office headquarters for international corporations, or housing and amenities for the masses.

Like many of the arts, architecture in the 20th century has sometimes appeared perilously close to self-destruction, and certainly in the last few decades has fragmented into increasingly numerous 'isms'.

The story of 20th-century architecture is primarily, however, the story of the modern movement. Modernism spent the early part of the century finding its feet, the middle asserting itself, and in latter years has been fighting a rearguard action in order to survive against the swing of popular opinion.

After trying so hard to shake off the legacy of a tradition that stretches back to classical times, architecture now finds itself steering an uneven path, pulled in one direction by the children of Modernism, and in the opposite direction by those who would see a return to historical roots. Perhaps the true judge of the 20th century will be time itself, and its verdict will be delivered in the extent to which Modernism survives into the next millenium.

LEFT **Hongkong & Shanghai Bank, Hong Kong, Foster Associates, 1981–85**
More than any other building, Norman Foster's skeletal High-Tech skyscraper represents the architecture of the 1980s.

TOP **Carson Pirie Scott department store, Chicago, Louis Sullivan, 1899–1904**
For Sullivan, even the relatively subtle expression of the building's cellular structure was a bold gesture.

ABOVE **Crystal Palace, London, Sir Joseph Paxton, 1851**
Not even recognized as architecture in its day, Crystal Palace was prophetic of Modernism in its use of prefabricated components and its rational solution to a problem.

KARLSPLATZ

1900
1918

INTRODUCTION

At the turn of the 20th century, the roots of modern architecture had already been planted in the steel-framed, multistorey commercial buildings by Louis Sullivan, Henry H Richardson and others, mainly in Chicago, St Louis and Buffalo, in the 1880s and 1890s. But it was to take another 20-odd years, and a war that was to change the world, before the spirit of 'Modernism' began to find a coherent style that it could call its own.

The years between were a time of experimentation, of ideas that veered between unprecedented social responsibility and escapist fantasy, and often of retreat into traditional ways. But the ground covered in the pre-World War I years was as great as that covered in entire centuries before.

During the 19th century, a number of factors conspired to create the pressure for a modern style of architecture. Continuing industrialization led to a need for new kinds of buildings, while the rapid growth in urban populations obliged architects to build upwards. Political reforms and the growing popularity of socialist ideals led people to question established values in every aspect of life, and to look for new artistic forms that expressed the changes in human society. By the end of the century, the materials and technology necessary to create a new architecture were also available.

The use of prefabricated cast-iron and wrought-iron components had been mastered by the middle of the century, in such buildings as Joseph Paxton's 1851 Crystal Palace in London. By the 1880s, Bessemer's new smelting techniques had enabled steel frames to be easily manufactured. Electric elevators, essential to transport people quickly up and down the new skyscrapers, were in operation by the 1890s. Most important of all, though, was the development of reinforced concrete, largely the work of François Hennebique in France, Reinforced concrete enabled huge distances to be spanned, and allowed construction of many buildings that would otherwise have been impossible.

By the start of the 20th century, the architectural establishment was ripe for change. For too long it had been dominated by historicism – the routine and often academic imitation of historical styles, with an emphasis on ornamentation. Britain's Arts and Crafts movement, in its quest to rediscover the simplicity of vernacular architecture, had been the first attempt to break the hold of historicism.

Art Nouveau became the first reaction on an international scale. Although with hindsight it may be regarded as a false start, there is no doubting the liberating effect that it achieved.

The world was entering a new era of communication heralded by developments like the invention of the wireless telegraph. This ensured that those engaged in the search for a modern style of architecture from as far afield as Chicago and Vienna, from Darmstadt to Barcelona, would be kept abreast of the changes in each other's countries.

OPPOSITE **Casa Milá, Barcelona, Antoní Gaudí, 1905**
Gaudí continued to create his own liberating form of Art Nouveau – the first movement to challenge the domination of historicism on an international scale – long after the style had died out in the rest of Europe.

RIGHT **Paris Opera House, Charles Garnier, 1861–75**
While applauded for its sense of occasion and ingenious use of a difficult site, Garnier's Baroque extravaganza epitomized the historicism propogated by the Ecole des Beaux Arts.

ART NOUVEAU

Art Nouveau was an international reaction against the backward-looking historicism that had passed for 19th-century architecture. Inspired by the imagery of organic structures like plant-forms and marine life, Art Nouveau was characterized by sinuous, curving lines that appeared in various undulating and interlaced patterns. It was a style that was readily adopted in many branches of design including textiles, glassware and jewelry. To its supporters it represented a daring challenge to the architectural establishment's sterile practice of endlessly reviving Renaissance and Classical styles. To its detractors, it seldom overcame the charge of being mere surface decoration, and was unworthy of the status of a truly architectural movement.

The origins of Art Nouveau lay mainly in Britain, where the Victorian ornamental designer Christopher Dresser was one of the first to recognize the potency of eccentric curves. In 1862 he wrote: 'A section of the outline of an ellipse is a more beautiful curve than that of the arc since its origin is less apparent, being traced from two centres.'

By common consensus, the first true example of Art Nouveau design was the title page by Arthur Mackmurdo (1851–1942) for his book *Wren's City Churches*, published in 1883. The floral designs of William Morris and the Arts and Crafts movement were also influential in formulating the Art Nouveau look.

OPPOSITE ABOVE **Castel Béranger, Paris, Hector Guimard, 1895–8**
Guimard readily adopted the whiplash line pioneered by Horta, and in this Paris apartment block he used cast plaster as well as iron for decoration.

OPPOSITE BELOW LEFT **Title page for *Wren's City Churches*, Arthur Mackmurdo, 1883**
The flame-like tendrils of Mackmurdo's illustration had an almost violent quality that was modified by many of his subsequent followers.

OPPOSITE BELOW RIGHT **Maison et Atelier Horta, Brussels, Victor Horta, 1898–1900**
Horta built himself a house and studio adjacent to each other in the rue Americaine in Brussels. Of the two, the house has the more remarkable exterior, with its elaborate ironwork balconies. Inside the studio (LEFT), Horta demonstrated his prowess at staircases with a typically elegant but fragile banister rail.

Art Nouveau became the basis for an international style largely through its dissemination in magazines, exhibitions and theoretical writings, all of which helped to bring together the isolated work of designers in a number of countries.

The name Art Nouveau was taken from a shop opened by the art dealer Samuel Bing in Paris in 1895, while the Italians dubbed it 'Stile Liberty' after Arthur Liberty's famous department store in London. In Germany and Scandinavia, it became known as 'Jugendstil' after the magazine *Jugend* which, together with the British *The Studio*, was responsible for exposing many Art Nouveau designs to a wider audience.

Although the origins of Art Nouveau may be found in Britain, it came to be regarded largely as a continental style, and one that was the object of some disdain in Britain. Nowhere was this more true than in the field of architecture, whose chief exponents of the style were to be found in Belgium, France and Spain.

The first buildings to be influenced by Art Nouveau appeared at the end of the 1880s. Although the United States never entered the mainstream of the Art Nouveau style, the spiky floral decorations for the 4,000-seat Chicago Auditorium in 1889 by Louis Sullivan (1856–1924) showed that the look had crossed the Atlantic even at that early stage.

It was in the fast-expanding Belgian capital of Brussels, through the works of Victor Horta (1861–1947), that an architectural style began to evolve. Horta's Hotel Tassel, designed in 1892, featured exposed floral ironwork and used linear tendril decoration on both walls and ceilings.

Having mastered the 'whiplash' line, Horta applied it extensively – notably in staircases – in buildings such as the Hotel Solvay (1894) and the Maison and Atelier Horta (1898–1900). At the same time, his structural and exterior design became increasingly adventurous. The Maison du Peuple of 1897 balanced the ele-

LEFT **Casa Batlló, Barcelona, Antoní Gaudí, 1905**
Gaudí created a new façade to an existing building for the cloth merchant José Battló. The result is a building that looks almost organic – it is difficult in places to distinguish the real windows from the bizarre balconies and surrounds.

ABOVE **Paris Métro entrance, Hector Guimard c1900**
Guarded by a pair of triffid-like lamp stems, it is not surprising that these subway entrances have had an unsettling effect on some Parisians.

ments of interlaced ironwork and elliptical windows in a sweeping concave façade. Horta's 'A l'Innovation' department store in 1901 was even more dramatic, presenting a soaring vertical composition of glass and curved ironwork to the street.

Another Belgian, Henri Van de Velde (1863–1957), first experimented with the Art Nouveau style through typography and book decoration. He progressed to interior decoration with the Hotel Otlet in 1894, and a year later built his own house at Bloemenwerf near Uccle. In marked contrast to Horta's flamboyant townhouses, it incorporated Art Nouveau lines into a rural idiom with striped gables and shuttered windows.

Van de Velde went on to design interiors for Bing's Paris shop before moving to Germany. There he set up the Weimar School of Arts and Crafts, which subsequently became the Bauhaus.

In France, the official training college for architects, designers and fine-arts students – the Ecole des Beaux-Arts – represented the historicizing tendency at its coldest and most academic. The compulsion to imitate is encapsulated in Charles Garnier's Paris Opera House, built between 1861 and 1875, which is regarded by its more vehement critics as a worthless exercise in plagiarism. However, France also had one radical thinker in the shape of the theorist Eugène Viollet-le-Duc (1814–79), who proposed a new 'rationalist' approach to architecture based upon rediscovering Gothic principles of constructing ribbed vaults, only using iron. Viollet-le-Duc went against the establishment view in preaching that iron should be used 'honestly', and left exposed, rather than hiding it with terracotta and other fake masonry.

His theories were to prove particularly influential to French architects of Art Nouveau. Of these, the greatest exponent was Hector Guimard (1867–1942), who designed the entrances for the Paris Métro system as well as a number of prominent houses. His Castel Béranger, finished in 1898, deployed floral motifs quite reminiscent of Horta, and indeed followed a visit to Belgium. Unlike Horta, however, Guimard worked in cast as well as wrought-iron, and it was the former that provided the basic material for the numerous Métro entrances and ticket offices he designed from 1900.

The entrances were inspired works of fantasy, consisting typically of a gateway over which the Métropolitain sign was suspended, abutted on either side by giant stems topped with flower-head lamps. The contrast these works often provided to the historical dignity of the buildings in front of which they stood infuriated many.

While best-known for his Métro designs, Guimard's masterpiece was the Humbert de Romans concert hall, built in 1898 and destroyed just seven years later as Art Nouveau quickly went out of fashion. Its crowning glory was a domed roof composed of steel ribs supporting a cupola pierced with windows of yellow stained glass.

Aside from Guimard and his contemporaries working in Paris, France had a second school of Art Nouveau architects working at Nancy in eastern France, at a colony led by the glassmaker

Glasgow School of Art, Charles Rennie Mackintosh, 1896–1908
Mackintosh's most original building. The influence of Art Nouveau is in the detail, rather than the overall impression.

Emile Gallé. Its outstanding achievement was the Villa Majorelle of 1900, which was designed chiefly by Henri Sauvage.

In both Belgium and France, there were a number of architects working along similar lines, and Art Nouveau could lay claim to being a movement of sorts. In Spain, Antoní Gaudí (1852–1926) worked in virtual isolation, and his only direct influences came from reading the works of Viollet-le-Duc, Ruskin and others. Yet Gaudí was arguably the most original and accomplished of all Art Nouveau architects.

Born in Tarragona, Gaudí moved to Barcelona, the capital of Catalonia, around 1869, where he met his main patron, Eusebio Güell. Aside from the neo-Gothic theories of Viollet-le-Duc, he was influenced by traditional Moorish and Moroccan styles, and by a mission to create a new Catalan architecture. His buildings were consequently more exotic than those of his contemporaries in northern Europe.

Gaudí's first work was the Casa Vicens, built between 1878 and 1880, in which the most striking departure was the wrought-iron railings and gates modelled on a pattern of palm fronds. Five years later he started the Palacio Güell, an extravagant town-house in which decorative ironwork was accompanied by poly-chromatic glazed tiles and banded brickwork, and in which the first of Gaudí's parabolic arches and twisted roof protuberances appeared.

The chapel of Santa Coloma de Cervelló, begun in 1898,

OPPOSITE BELOW **Hill House, Helensburgh, Scotland, Charles Rennie Mackintosh, 1902–3**
Like the School of Art, Hill House has something of the Scottish castle about it, with its stark walls, grid-mullioned windows and its turret-like bay. It was built for the publisher Walter Blackie.

incorporated a fantastic, rather nightmarish interior in which jagged asymmetry was enhanced by leaning monolithic pillars, uneven vaults and a variety of raw textures and materials. This theme was continued in the Güell Parque of 1900, while Gaudí took the principles of Art Nouveau to their architectural extreme in two apartment blocks begun in 1905, the Casa Batlló and the Casa Milá. Though different, each building was distinguished by almost sculptural exterior surfaces of wave-like undulating masonry, punctuated by twisted wrought-iron balconies. Inside, there was not a single straight wall against which to place furniture. The two blocks represent the most convincing repudiation of the oft-levelled charge that Art Nouveau was mere surface decoration.

There is one other fiercely individual architect of this period whose name is often associated with Art Nouveau. Charles Rennie Mackintosh (1858–1928) built almost exclusively in and around the city of Glasgow, where he had studied at the art school, and then went on to experiment in designing graphics and metal-work.

Mackintosh's first important commission came in 1896, when he won a competition to design a new School of Art for the city. At first sight, the building which he constructed over 12 years bears little resemblance to Art Nouveau works elsewhere. Its grid-like mullioned windows, stark massive flank wall and roof-turrets betray influences ranging from English Tudor to Scottish baronial castles – and even Baroque. But the influence of Horta and Guimard can be detected in the general asymmetry, in the sparing use of elliptical curves, and in the delicate ironwork seen at its most original in the decoratively curled brackets set against the huge studio windows of the façade.

Unlike the Belgians and the French, Mackintosh used the languid curves of Art Nouveau with great austerity, and in harmonious counterpoint to grid-like patterns of horizontal and vertical lines. Although further buildings such as Hill House, Helensburgh, a series of tea-rooms for Mrs Cranston and Mackintosh's furniture designs all received attention in his lifetime, he achieved greater recognition in Germany and Austria (especially among the architects of the Secession) than he ever did in Britain. Mackintosh's greatest achievement may have been to point a path forward from the decorative excesses of Art Nouveau, which found itself in fading popularity after the first five years of the decade, and was laid to rest by the horrors of World War I.

AUSTRIA AND THE SECESSIONISTS

Just as the Arts and Crafts practitioners had lauded the merits of simplicity and honesty in architecture and design, so too did a number of architects working in Austria at the turn of the century. Loosely described as the 'Vienna School', the chief exponents were Otto Wagner (1841–1918), Joseph Olbrich (1867–1908), Adolf Loos (1870–1933) and Josef Hoffmann (1870–1956).

Otto Wagner, the elder statesman of the group, published *Moderne Architektur* in 1895 in which he argued the case for architecture to respond to and reflect the more 'modern' life-style of the day. Similarly, the German architect August Endell wrote at this time of the need for a style of architecture to evolve, one that did not rely on historical precedent but that had an inherent purity of form. Of equal significance to these architects during this period, however, was the impact of the Art Nouveau movement in general and of Charles Rennie Mackintosh in particular.

The combination of such diverse influences produced a particularly curious hybrid architecture, seen as early as 1894–7 in Wagner's Karlsplatz Stadtbahn station: the steel-frame structure is an evident element, but floral decorative features predominate.

ABOVE & RIGHT **Post Office Savings Bank, Vienna, Otto Wagner, 1904–6**
A rarity in buildings of this period, aluminium is used extensively through the building (RIGHT) from the casing of structural supports to the sculpted figures which punctuate the façade. Wagner was also responsible for the design of the tables, chairs and other items. Shown here is the large central banking hall (ABOVE).

OPPOSITE **Karlsplatz station, Vienna Stadtbahn, Otto Wagner, 1894–7**
Wagner was commissioned to devise a scheme for the replanning of the centre of Vienna; the Stadtbahn was the sole element to come to fruition.

KARLSPLATZ

LEFT **Secession exhibition building, Vienna, JM Olbrich, 1897–9**
Olbrich was one of the founder members of the Wiener Secession for whom he designed this exhibition hall. The metalwork is alive with organic animal and plant life, softening the overall monumentality of the building.

OPPOSITE ABOVE **Palais Stoclet, Brussels, Belgium, Josef Hoffmann, 1905–11**
With a large budget at his disposal, Hoffmann was able to use the best materials. Various marbles are used throughout the interior and the dining-room is decorated with panels by Gustav Klimt.

OPPOSITE BELOW **Steiner house, Vienna, Adolf Loos, 1910**
This view of the back of the building reveals Loos' rejection of ornament in favour of bare concrete, plate-glass windows and a flat roof. The creeper helps soften the otherwise harsh exterior.

The dichotomy is further expressed in Olbrich's Wiener Secession exhibition building completed in 1899. Olbrich had been one of the founders of the breakaway Wiener Secession in 1897 and, as such, felt it necessary to make a strong architectural statement. The main structure of the building is substantial, complete with concrete facing, but the detailing with animal and vegetable life is an all-important aspect of the building, particularly on the metal tracery of the iron dome. Like the spires of Cologne's medieval cathedral, the perforated structure lightens the 'weight' of the building.

The speed with which Art Nouveau was acknowledged was equalled only by the speed with which it came under criticism. Wagner's Post Office Savings Bank built between 1904 and 1906 in the centre of Vienna, reveals a completely new aesthetic, based soundly on 'truth to materials' with its austere ornament. Like the high-tech work of Piano & Rogers and Norman Foster many years later, structural components such as rivets and nuts provide a wealth of decoration. Here, Wagner created a building using up-to-date methods of construction and materials such as steel, aluminium, glass and concrete to create a large airy main hall. To the contemporary eye the interior of the building must have appeared somewhat spartan. (As if a token gesture to public sentiment, the façade is topped by a pair of large statues.) However far the reduction to structural essentials had been taken, the proportions of the building, both inside and out, owe much to the Classical conventions of order and symmetry.

Josef Hoffmann, a former pupil of Wagner's at the Vienna Akademie's school of architecture, appreciated craftsmanship and believed that ornament had an important role in architecture. Together with Koloman Moser, he established the Wiener

Werkstatte, a workshop dedicated to the production of functional but beautiful objects.

Hoffmann's Purkersdorf convalescent home (1903) reveals structural sincerity; his designs for the Palais Stoclet in Brussels (1905–11), however, allowed him to put his theories fully into practise. Stoclet, a wealthy financier, commissioned Hoffmann to build a palatial home that should also serve as a suitable setting for his art collection and for entertaining. What Hoffmann designed was a house of great distinction, combining elements of formality (strong horizontals and verticals) with great informality (an irregular floor plan and a façade that did nothing to hide the irregularity of the room arrangement within). The asymmetry of the design coupled with the unusual shapes and positions of the windows points strongly to Mackintosh's work.

Adolf Loos' sources of inspiration were further afield: he greatly admired Roman architecture, and inherited from his stone-mason father a deep respect for 'raw' materials. He travelled to the United States in 1893, the year after Louis Sullivan had published his 'Ornament in Architecture'. Three years later he settled in Vienna, bringing with him a belief in the rejection of ornament (summed up in his essay entitled 'Ornament and Crime' of 1908). Perhaps because of his outspoken stance, large-scale commissions were slow to come, his most notable piece of design during this early period being the Kärntner Bar of 1907. The apparent harshness of its geometric order is dissolved by the richness of shiny metals and lavish leather seating.

Loos designed a house for the Steiner family in Vienna in 1910 and this commission provided him with the opportunity to manifest his principles. The house is outstanding, not least because it is one of the first examples of domestic architecture to use reinforced concrete. Externally, the building consists of smooth, flat walls of solid geometric blocks pierced by plate-glass windows (many horizontal) and a flat roof. Internally, the same geometric order prevails, but around an essentially traditional plan. Loos went on to design many private villas, finally settling in Paris, where he designed a house for the Dadaist, Tristan Tzara, in 1926.

ABOVE **The Ward Willitts house, Highland Park, Illinois, Frank Lloyd Wright, 1902**
The bold geometry of this façade, created by wooden beams breaking the white paintwork, bears witness to Wright's interest in Japanese architecture. He used stained glass in many of his early houses to create coloured light effects inside.

RIGHT **The Robie house, Chicago, Illinois, Frank Lloyd Wright, 1907–9**
Marking the climax of Wright's Prairie Style houses, the Robie house was constructed out of Roman brick. The deep overhang contains a steel supporting arm.

FRANK LLOYD WRIGHT AND DOMESTIC STYLE

Frank Lloyd Wright (1867–1959) designed many buildings over a period of more than 60 years, from small modular houses, suburban palaces and factories, to churches and art galleries. His work is particularly important because of its influence on other architects practising throughout the 20th century. His genius sprang not just from his ability to design buildings that were pleasing to the eye and to the environment, nor from his ability to create an interesting interior ground plan, but predominantly from his intuitive skill in combining all these elements into organically unified buildings.

Wright studied engineering at the University of Wisconsin in Madison before briefly joining the practice of John Lyman Silsbee, an exponent of the 'Shingle Style' of architecture. This style is epitomized by works of generously sized domestic architecture which rely on open ground-plans and quality craftsmanship in their construction. Such principles appealed to Wright's appre-

ABOVE **The Gamble house, Pasadena, California, Charles & Henry Greene, 1908–9**
The Greenes were meticulous about the quality of workmanship that went into the houses they designed and their furnishings. Their houses of this period display a peculiar mixture of Tyrolean chalet and American Shingle style forms.

ciation of all things from nature. Other early influences were Ruskin and the Arts and Crafts movement, as well as traditional Japanese architecture. In 1887 he joined the leading Chicago architectural practice of Louis Sullivan (1856–1924) and Dankmar Adler (1844–1900). This firm's use of skeletal construction coupled with organic ornamentation were manifested in the Wainwright Building in St Louis (1890–1).

Wright set up a studio in 1889 in Oak Park, a wealthy suburb of Chicago and spent much of the next 15 years designing and developing Prairie Style houses, many for patrons who lived in the immediate vicinity. The term 'Prairie' is derived from one of two designs that he had published in 1901 in the *Ladies' Home Journal* entitled 'A Home in a Prairie Town'. (The other design was called 'A Small House with Lots of Room in it'.) This design reveals many of the hallmarks that typify Wright's Prairie Style houses of this period – an asymmetrical ground-plan, a façade that reflects the arrangements of the rooms within, strong horizontal elements, shallow roofs with overhanging eaves and many screen-like windows. Inside, the focal point of the house is undoubtedly the fireplace, with strong axial lines running across the house. Above all, the house is designed to be lived in: from the built-in furniture to the deep eaves for keeping the house cool, the house is supremely practical.

The Ward Willitts house (1902) is situated in Highland Park on the outskirts of Chicago and displays many of the Prairie Style characteristics but blended with strong Japanese overtones. Like much of Wright's work during this period, the house is devoid of unnecessary ornament, with strong grid-like black-and-white façades which are not uncomfortable in the surrounding area. The basement, so prevalent in American suburban houses, has

OPPOSITE ABOVE **Unity Church, Oak Park, Chicago, Illinois, Frank Lloyd Wright, 1906**
This building was made primarily of concrete and coated with a special pebble aggregate. The primitive South American-inspired ornament is integral to the building.

OPPOSITE BELOW **The Walter Dodge house, Los Angeles, California, Irving Gill, 1915–6, demolished**
Gill's proto-Modernist style featured smooth stucco walls with large windows and little decorative detailing.

ABOVE **Interior of Unity Church, Oak Park, Chicago, Illinois, Frank Lloyd Wright, 1906**
Wright designed the interiors, including furniture and light fittings, for many of his buildings. The 'graphic' quality of this interior is heightened by the decorative lines.

been raised out of the ground, creating a podium for the floors above. Many years later Wright attempted to analyze his guiding beliefs behind the designs of these early houses and, above all else, he deemed unity – both in relation to interior spaces and in relation to the house and its environment – as a prime objective.

One of the strongest examples of Wright's Prairie Style is the house he designed for a businessman called Frederick C Robie in 1907. Situated in a relatively built-up area of Chicago, the house occupies a tight corner site. Wright's solution was to impose one giant slab of the building on top (but shifted across) of another; the top slab housed the living rooms out of sight from passers-by, whereas the lower slab housed the children's playroom and the billiards room. The longitudinal thrust of the house is further emphasized by extended overhangs on the outside (supported by a steel beam at one point), and by an open and flowing living space (combining the living and dining rooms) on the inside. Whereas earlier Wright houses may have incorporated somewhat 'relaxed' ground-plans, the Robie House manifested a complete departure from more formalized arrangements.

In addition to his predominantly domestic commissions, Wright received several other offers of work during this period, including the opportunity to design a church complex in his own neighbourhood of Oak Park, Chicago (1906). He managed to convince his patrons, the Unitarians, to abandon the traditional basilica plan and, in its place, he created a squarish meeting hall. Like many of Wright's buildings, his brilliance in manipulating space within this church and the attached meeting area is hard to appreciate without actually standing within them. The design is based on squares and rectangles, a formula that is carried throughout the building, including the light fittings. Most important, however, is Wright's use of concrete on the exterior of the building, which is surfaced with a pebble aggregate. Such an unashamed use of this material was very unusual for works of architecture as opposed to engineering, and looks forward to the next decade.

Other architects who produced their own variations of the Shingle Style include Charles (1868–1957) and Henry (1870–1954) Greene. Having worked in Massachusetts (and having seen the work of H H Richardson), they worked extensively in California, absorbing the West Coast wooden style of architecture into their work. The Gamble house in Pasadena (1908–9) shows many characteristics of their style at this time – a long, low façade, redwood construction, balconies and deep overhanging eaves. Like Wright, the Greenes used stained glass to enrich the interiors of their houses, and also supervised meticulously the construction of all their designs.

Another Californian architect working in the years leading up to World War I who anticipated some of the principles of the Modern Movement was Irving Gill (1870–1936). Gill appreciated the simplicity of concrete, and he designed geometric, white buildings devoid of ornament that, although hardly known in Europe, looked towards the Modernism of the 1920s and '30s.

THE BRITISH TRADITION

At the turn of the century, as Art Nouveau luxuriated fashionably through much of Europe, Britain continued to go its own way, with innovation in architecture dominated by the dual themes of Arts and Crafts and the English Domestic Revival.

While European designers were happy to acknowledge their debt to Art Nouveau's British origins, it never caught on seriously as an architectural style in Britain, where a more simple, less decorative style was favoured.

This tradition, encompassing both Arts and Crafts and the revival of vernacular house styles, originated with the Red House at Bexleyheath, built by Philip Webb (1831–1915) in 1859 for William Morris. In its honest presentation of brick and woodwork and the free hand with which it incorporated period details, the Red House was quite revolutionary. At the same time, it was comfortable and cosy in the tradition of old English country houses.

Webb's liberated approach to using historic precedent was taken up by his contemporary Richard Norman Shaw (1831–1912) who, together with William Nesfield, evolved the 'Queen Anne' style that characterizes Shaw's most successful buildings. In his New Zealand Chambers in the City of London and Old Swan House in Chelsea, Shaw combined elements from the 17th and 18th centuries such as oriel windows, ornate mouldings and unrendered brickwork to achieve a result that was at once delicate and domestic.

BELOW **St Osmund's Church, Poole, Dorset, Edward Schroeder Prior**

OPPOSITE **The Red House, Bexleyheath, Kent, Philip Webb, 1859**
One of the important early buildings of the English Domestic Revival, The Red House brought back simplicity in the form of a cosy grouping around a well.

Although Shaw turned on occasion to William Morris's company to provide interior decoration for his buildings, he remained largely outside the Arts and Crafts movement. However, it was a group of Shaw's assistants who in 1884 were instrumental in forming the Art Workers Guild, which became a central forum for Arts and Crafts ideas in architecture. Among them were Edward Schroeder Prior (1852–1932) and William Lethaby (1857–1931), two of the most ardent supporters of Morris's philosophy. Prior was an outspoken advocate of the need to return to natural materials, which he saw as a means to deflate the pomposity of much Victorian architecture. He used a range of local materials including sandstone, flint, pebbles and brick in an attempt to recreate a vernacular style in houses like The Barn in Exmouth, Devon, huge and thatched, and the more exotic Home Place in Norfolk.

Prior's contemporary Lethaby was similarly inspired by Morris and Webb, but his contribution as a writer and educator was probably greater than that as a working architect. Lethaby became the first principal of the London Central School of Arts and Crafts in 1900, where he set up craft workshops and later argued the need for industrial design. Lethaby's most important building was ironically a church – All Saints at Brockhampton in

RIGHT **Walnut Tree Farm, Castlemorton, Worcestershire, Charles Annesley Voysey, 1890** One of Voysey's earlier houses, it already shows the low, gabled roofs, narrow horizontal windows and broad tapering chimney-stack that Voysey made his hallmark.

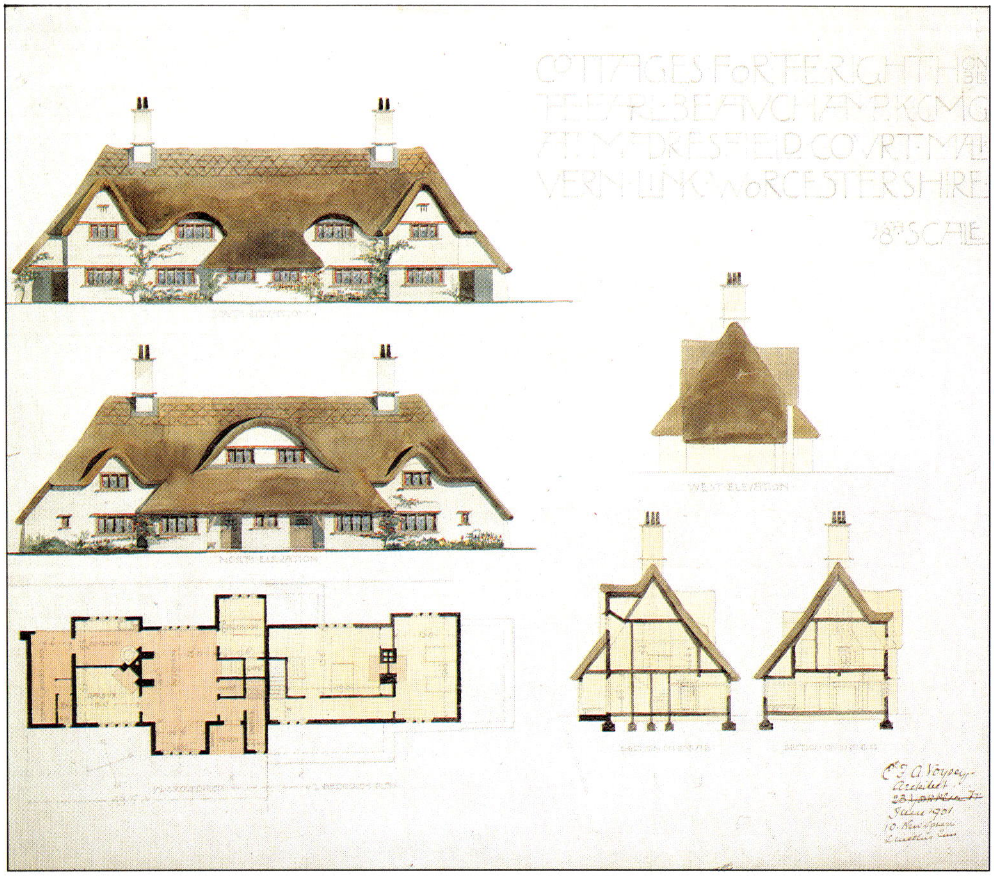

BELOW **Drawings for cottages at Madresfield Court, Worcestershire, Charles Annesley Voysey, 1901** These cottages for the Earl of Beauchamp are unusual for Voysey in having thatched roofs, but otherwise retain the typical lowslung look, which is a feature of his work.

OPPOSITE **The Orchard, Chorleywood, Hertfordshire, Charles Annesley Voysey, 1899** Voysey built The Orchard for himself and expended a great deal of energy on the interior decoration, which included his highly original wallpaper.

Herefordshire – whose traditional thatched exterior masked the startling concrete tunnel vault within.

Where Lethaby was sparse in his output, Charles Annesley Voysey (1857–1941) was prolific. He designed some 40 houses between 1889 and 1910, ensuring his place as the most accomplished exponent of domestic architecture in the two decades around the turn of the century. Voysey joined the Art Workers Guild several years after its foundation, but he remained a staunch puritan in philosophy, building houses with an austere simplicity that would, in fact, become his strength.

Voysey's houses closely adhered to a basic style that comprised overhanging slate roofs, rough-cast rendered walls, horizontal windows with unmoulded mullions, and huge tapering chimney-stacks. These elements were organized in a low, spreading arrangement reminiscent of Frank Lloyd Wright's Prairie Style houses, but with little experimentation in the use of interior space. Voysey was renowned for designing his houses to take

some detail of the location into account, such as the sunlight, the view, or even a tree.

The demand for comfortable country houses of modest size was fuelled at this time by the creation of a new middle class, and owed much to the wealth generated as people cashed in their government bonds after the Boer War (1899–1902). Voysey was the most successful of a group of architects who met this demand. Another was Hugh Mackay Baillie Scott, who attracted widespread attention abroad, most notably in Germany, where he was commissioned to decorate some rooms in the Grand Duke of Hesse's palace at Darmstadt. Baillie Scott's architectural style owed a good deal to Voysey, but he was more adventurous in his use of interior space, experimenting with double-height hallways and rooms arranged in a sequence that encouraged fluid movement between them.

Another skilled architect of country houses, albeit on a slightly grander scale than Voysey, was Edwin Lutyens (1869–1944), who was firmly ensconced in the Arts and Crafts movement at the turn of the century. Lutyens was renowned for wit and inventiveness in his early houses, often in collaboration with the garden designer Gertrude Jekyll. An example of dramatic manipulation was Tigbourne Court in Surrey, an almost theatrical composition in masonry.

The war in 1914 shattered the dream-like world of the leisured rich for whom Lutyens had built, and the harsh realism of industrialized warfare also put paid to the medievalist innocence of Arts and Crafts. But while the days of individually commissioned country houses were largely over, some trace of the designs of Voysey and Baillie Scott would reappear in debased form in the suburbs of mock-Tudor housing that sprang up between the world wars.

Although the preoccupation of architects in Britain before 1914 was mainly with commissions for the wealthy classes, Britain's Garden City movement in the same period placed it ahead of other European countries in pioneering well-designed, environmentally attractive housing for the working class. Paternalistic manufacturers had built garden cities for their employees at Bournville, Birmingham, and Port Sunlight, Liverpool, in the late 19th century, but what Ebenezer Howard proposed in 1898 was an enlightened programme of new towns based on development in the countryside, in the spirit of the Arts and Crafts movement.

Under Howard's influence, Barry Parker and Raymond Unwin planned Letchworth Garden City, begun in 1903, and the more 'up-market' Hampstead Garden Suburb in 1907, the latter with the help of Lutyens. Both developments reproduced elements of Webb and Shaw on a large scale, in rows of picturesque cottage-style housing.

But despite the initial success, Howard's hope that people would abandon the overcrowded cities to rediscover a self-regulated semi-rural existence was to prove something of a pipedream in the 20th century.

LEFT **Castle Drogo, Drewsteignton, Devon, Edwin Lutyens, 1910–30**
One of the most original of Lutyens' country houses, Castle Drogo was built for the wealthy Drew family.

TOP **Waterlow Court, Hampstead Garden Suburb, London, Hugh Mackay Baillie Scott, 1909**
A development of single flats for working women, built around a cloistered courtyard.

ABOVE **Letchworth Garden City, Hertfordshire, Barry Parker and Raymond Unwin, 1903**
In Letchworth, the first of the true Garden Cities, houses were surrounded by continuous grass verges and herbaceous borders.

NEW IDEAS

In the years before World War I, the search for a 'modern' style preoccupied architects in Europe and America, and led to a good deal of experimentation. Primarily it was a question of experimenting with the new materials – concrete, steel frames, plate-glass, light alloys and aluminium – but some architects were also concerned with planning the cities of the future.

The most important material of the modern era was reinforced concrete, and one of the first buildings to be made with a framework composed entirely of the new material was the Rue Franklin apartment building in Paris, constructed between 1902 and 1904 by Auguste Perret (1874–1954). The framework was clearly expressed on the front of the building, even though it was covered with terracotta tiles. The plain tiles chosen for the skeleton contrasted with the floral designs used for infill panels on the non-structural parts of the façade. In his next Paris building, a garage in the rue Ponthieu (1905–6), Perret was more adventurous, leaving the concrete supports uncovered but for a coat of white paint, and using them to frame huge windows.

Perret's other pre-war building was the Théâtre des Champs-Elysées, in which Perret took over the commission from Henrí Van de Velde. Although the frame was again of concrete, it was considered unbecoming for this to be seen on a theatre, so the façade was faced with stone.

In Germany, meanwhile, Peter Behrens (1868–1940) was the first leading designer and architect to look beyond Art Nouveau.

In 1907, Behrens was appointed as architect to the giant electrical company AEG, and in the ensuing two years he built a huge turbine assembly shop for the company in Berlin.

This building was something of a landmark in the design of factories, which had hitherto been regarded as strictly utilitarian in their requirements. Behrens' factory introduced a sense of monumentality through the combination of massive concrete corners and subtly sloping glass curtain walls. The design also alluded to the past through its resemblance to a traditional gabled barn. Two years after its completion, Behrens' work was followed by Walter Gropius (1883–1969) and Adolf Meyer's Fagus factory at Alfeld-an-der-Leine, which took the curtain walls one stage further, completely abolishing blind corners.

Behrens went on to design an inventive complex of water and gas works at Frankfurt-am-Main, which was completed in 1912, and he was an important influence on Gropius, Mies van der Rohe and Le Corbusier, each of whom worked for him during this period.

Another architect who made an important contribution to the development of industrial buildings was Hans Poelzig (1869–1936), who practised in Breslau after studying in Berlin. Poelzig built a water tower at Posen (Poznan) in 1911 which doubled as an exhibition centre, complete with restaurant. The water tower was a seven-sided steel-framed structure of brick and glass, and like Behrens' AEG factory, it had aesthetic as well as utilitarian value. The following year, 1912, Poëlzig completed a chemical factory at Luban, in which he explored the way that buildings of different shapes and sizes could be arranged together to give a sense of unity.

Poelzig also constructed an office building in Breslau (Wroczlaw) between 1911 and 1912 in which horizontal bands of windows alternated with a continuous cornice of concrete, a stylistic motif

OPPOSITE ABOVE **Glass House, Bruno Taut, Werkbund Exhibition, Cologne, 1914**
Even the stairs were made of glass blocks in this futuristic homage to the material which became an obsession for Taut.

OPPOSITE BELOW **Luban Chemical Works, Hans Poelzig, 1912**
Poelzig's factory has none of the lightness of some of the other industrial buildings being designed at the time but is interesting for its deployment of varied shapes and textures.

RIGHT **AEG Turbine Factory, Berlin, Peter Behrens, 1909**
The turbine hall was just one of the products of Behrens' collaboration with AEG, which saw him design a range of appliances for the company such as lamps, electric fans and kettles.

that became widely used by architects of commercial buildings such as Mies van der Rohe in the 1920s and 1930s.

While Behrens and Poelzig were striving after a new form for industrial architecture, Bruno Taut (1880–1938) was concerned with exploring the possibilities of materials. His Steel Industry Pavilion at the Leipzig Fair of 1913 was followed by the much more dramatic Glass House at the Werkbund Exhibition at Cologne the following year. Consisting of a prismatic dome on top of a cylindrical drum, the building surface consisted almost entirely of glass, and foreshadowed the technique of Richard Buckminster Fuller's 'geodesic' domes of the 1950s. It was inscribed with aphorisms by the poet Paul Scheerbart such as 'Light wants crystal' and 'Without a glass palace, life becomes a burden', giving a hint of the utopian philosophy that Taut was to formulate more fully after World War I.

By 1913, ten years after Perret's first concrete-framed apartment block, there were already great advances being made in the use of reinforced concrete. In that year, Max Berg completed the first large-scale dome to be constructed from the new material in his Centennial Hall at Breslau (Wroczlaw). The central auditorium was spanned by a dome 213 feet (65m) in diameter, which was supported by 32 concrete ribs. In 1916, the engineer Eugène Freyssinet began building two airship hangars at Orly, each over 200 feet (61m) high. They took the form of concrete barrel vaults, and created an immense covered space.

While many progressive architects were busy experimenting with materials and designing buildings of the future, there were others who were concerned with planning the cities that would

ABOVE **Drawings for *La Città Nuova*, Antonio Sant'Elia, 1913** Sant'Elia's vision provides a foretaste of the Brutalism to come 50 years later, but also shows carefully considered details, such as the extensive pedestrian walkways.

BELOW **Airship hangars at Orly, France, Eugène Freyssinet, 1916** These giant hangars – each 985 ft (300 m) long – were made of prefabricated components and were entirely self-supporting. They were dismantled after the war.

accommodate them. The French architect Tony Garnier (1869–1948) produced his designs for the 'Cité Industrielle' after winning the Prix de Rome in 1899. Conceived as an industrial city of 35,000 inhabitants, Garnier's scheme was the first truly detailed blueprint of the 'modern' city, right down to the locations of housing, factories, railways and hospitals. It was exhibited in 1904 and published in 1917, and although Garnier was able to realize some of his ideas with buildings in his native Lyon, the Cité Industrielle remained a set of plans.

Antonio Sant'Elia (1880–1916) was an Italian architect allied to the Futurists – the Italian movement inspired by the poet Marinetti, which revered the machine. The Futurists' attitude was expressed by Marinetti with the words 'A roaring, racing car, rattling past like a machine gun, is more beautiful than the Winged Victory of Samothrace'. Sant'Elia's own vision of the city of the future was contained in a set of drawings, *La Città Nuova*, published in 1913. It incorporated bold ideas such as soaring skyscrapers with receding upper floors to allow more light onto the streets, and pedestrian walkways that spanned sunken freeways. Sant'Elia was killed in action in 1916, and his plans were never put into construction. But like those of Garnier, they proved highly influential when modern cities were eventually built.

LEFT **Residential quarter from drawings for the *Cité Industrielle*, Tony Garnier, 1917**
Garnier predicted functional, cubic housing that would be set in a pedestrianized, landscaped residential quarter.

BELOW **General view of the hospital from drawings for the *Cité Industrielle*, Tony Garnier, 1917**
In Garnier's plan, the hospital was placed outside the town, well away from the centre of industry.

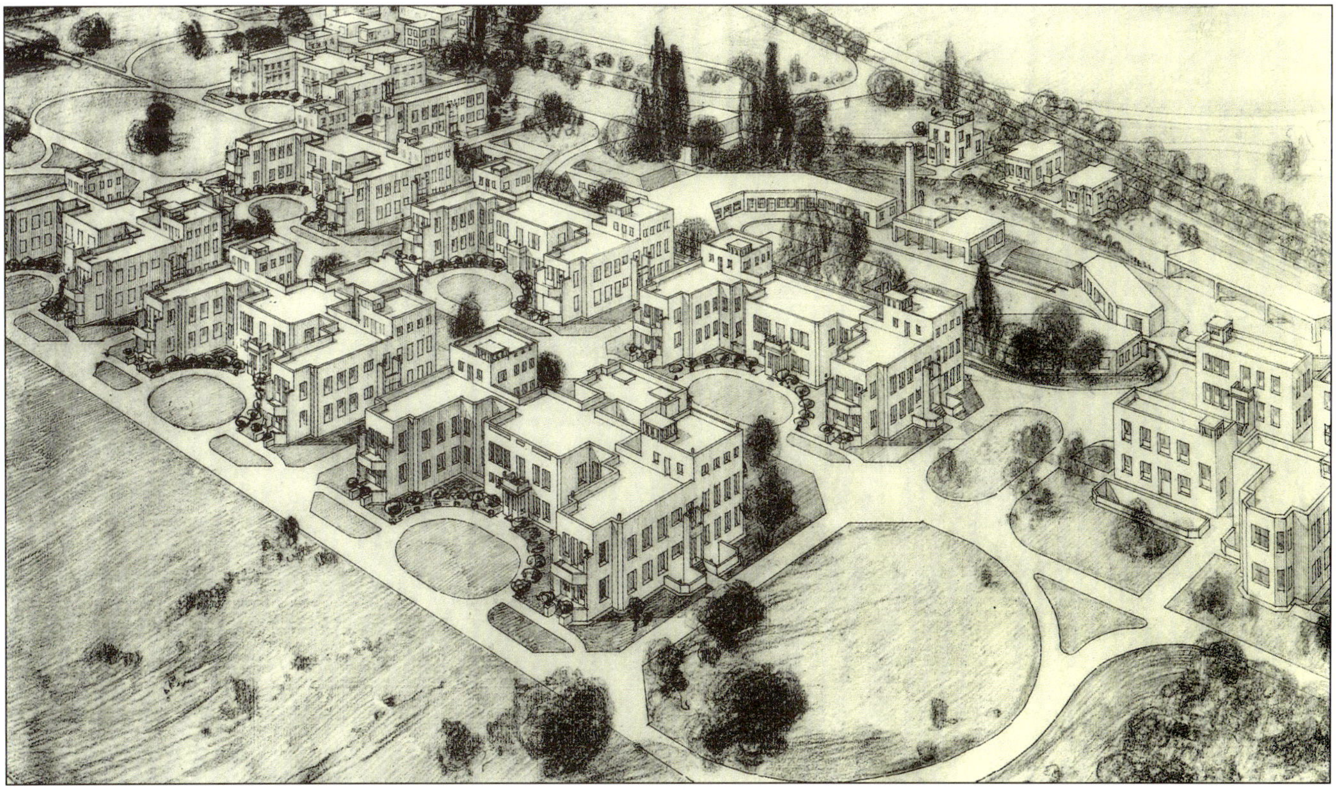

1918
1945

INTRODUCTION 1918–1945

Most countries in Europe were affected to varying degrees by World War I which raged from 1914 to 1918. Resources were diverted, not only in terms of raw materials but also in terms of manpower. Building, which is notoriously costly in both respects, was severely restricted. Rare exceptions during the period were the buildings constructed or converted for war-time use, such as Eugène Freyssinet's airship hangars begun at Orly in 1916 which were made from concrete and were spectacularly large.

The war left behind it the opportunity for building on an unprecedented scale. Factories and commercial buildings were needed to revitalize economies, and dwellings were needed for home-coming troops. The slogan was 'building a land fit for heroes', even if resources were somewhat restricted.

The manner and style of architecture produced in the years 1918 to 1945 varies enormously. Though highly significant to contemporary and future architecture, the International Style was developed and practised by a limited number of rarified architects and did not, in fact, cater for an audience beyond architectural-magazine readers until after World War II. Most architecture was fundamentally traditional, drawing on historical precedent for inspiration. State architecture, particularly in Hitler's Germany and Stalin's Russia, remained predominantly neo-Classical in spirit. Ranging from Lutyens' Viceroy's House in New Delhi (1913–29) to Henry Bacon's Lincoln Memorial in Washington (1911–22), the style was suitable for governments endeavouring to imply strength and control through their buildings.

Commercial architecture utilized any number of styles to suit its purpose, chief among these being Art Deco and Art Moderne. These styles absorbed the principles of geometry and apparent simplicity from Modernism, but also concentrated on machines (and machine-made objects) for inspiration. They were styles that not only affected entire buildings, such as the Hoover Factory in London designed by Wallis Gilbert and Partners (1932–5), but also lent themselves to surface treatment with the result that they were used widely for shop fronts.

Improvements in construction techniques, including the mastery of reinforced concrete, allowed architects to build ever bigger and higher. In the United States in particular, skyscrapers grew up in startling numbers in city centres such as Chicago and New York; the Wall Street Crash of 1929 and the subsequent depression only briefly affected their growth. It was steel that fundamentally allowed buildings to go higher; it also allowed wider expanses of glass to be used, a phenomenon that Mies van der Rohe explored in his German pavilion for the Barcelona Exhibition of 1929. As buildings went up, they also went outwards. New and better methods of transportation, particularly in local railway services, opened up the outlying areas around the big cities and towns to development, creating large tracts of planned suburbs in the United States and 'ribbon' developments in Britain.

Modern Movements

The search for a 'modern' architecture, which had plagued the more intellectually minded architects in the early years of the 20th century, crystallized in the years following the end of World War I in 1918. A handful of architects, working either on their own or in groups, provided their own interpretation of a building style for the future which had certain common characteristics. They were drawn from shared influences, the most important of which were the architecture of Frank Lloyd Wright, Cubist and Abstract art and the 'machine aesthetic' – and the subsequent reinterpretation of spatial relationships and the rationalization of construction methods. Loosely termed the International Style, it embraced such architects as Le Corbusier, the De Stijl group (notably van Doesburg and Rietveld), Walter Gropius, Konstantin Melnikov and Mies van der Rohe, and constituted the earliest form of Modernism.

In 1927 the Weissenhof Exhibition, at which many of these architects had exhibited, revealed the similarity of their approach and meaning. In the following year Hélène de Mandrot in association with Le Corbusier and Sigfried Giedion set up the Congrès Internationaux d'Architecture Moderne (CIAM), stating amongst other objectives: 'It is only from the present that our architectural work should be derived'. The organization turned its attentions towards town planning and 'habitat' early on, in hindsight the area where perhaps Modernism was to prove least successful.

OPPOSITE **Notre Dame, Le Raincy, near Paris, Auguste Perret, 1922–3**
With its basilica plan, slender columns and stained-glass windows, this church echoed Gothic architecture, but with one outstanding difference – it was made out of reinforced concrete. The stained glass was designed by Maurice Denis.

RIGHT **The Chrysler building, New York, William van Alen, 1928–30**
The metallic casing of this soaring edifice would seem to be entirely appropriate for the offices of one of America's leading automobile manufacturers. Giant metal radiator caps adorned the fortieth floor along with car wheels and hub-caps.

EXPRESSIONISM

The pioneer of Expressionism in architecture can be said to have been Antoní Gaudí in Barcelona, in his later works from about 1903, but as a movement it undoubtedly reached its apotheosis in Germany just before and after World War I.

Architectural Expressionism is characterized by the free use of abstract form, which is considered to take precedence over considerations of function or historical precedent.

In Gaudí's two late apartment blocks, the Casa Batlló (1907) and the Casa Milá (1910), he created an organic quality of undulating masonry that was closely linked to the Art Nouveau style.

The first appearance of Expressionist architecture in northern Europe was during World War I in Holland, where Michel de Klerk (1884–1923) and Piet Kramer (1881–1961) built a series of housing estates in Amsterdam which created unorthodox shapes out of brickwork. One of the best examples is de Klerk's Eigen Haard housing estate, built between 1913 and 1920, which made widespread use of rounded bricks to create curved corners and a curved tower.

In Germany, Expressionism arose largely as a reaction to the regulated style of the Werkbund, but it also became closely associated with the movement of Expressionism in fine arts, and particularly with the Dresden-based artists' group Die Brücke.

After the war, Expressionist ideas were exchanged under the auspices of the 'Glass Chain', an informal group led by Bruno Taut who circulated letters to each other under pseudonyms. In 1919, Taut published a collection of drawings of utopian glass temples under the title *Alpine Architektur*. Another member of the 'Glass Chain', Hermann Finsterlin, published sketches and models that were even more fantastic.

Of the Expressionist architecture that was built, one of the best examples was Hans Poelzig's remodelling of the Grosses Schauspielhaus in Berlin for the theatrical director Max Reinhardt in 1919. It consisted of a 5,000-seat auditorium festooned with stalactites like an enormous fairy grotto. The hanging icicles were studded with reflectors which, when illuminated before a performance, were designed to transport the audience into a dream-like world.

In 1921, Erich Mendelsohn (1887–1953) built an observatory and astrophysical laboratory at Potsdam, named in honour of Albert Einstein. Mendelsohn saw the 'Einstein House' as a chance to realize his ideas about the sculptural qualities of concrete, but he was forced to resort to plastered brickwork in some parts of its construction. The observatory was essentially a tower surmounted by a cupola, encased in a seemingly aerodynamic shell with recessed windows eerily reminiscent of human eyes.

Fritz Höger's (1877–1949) Chilehaus, an office building constructed in the centre of Hamburg in 1923, was built on a three-cornered site. Höger exploited this circumstance by developing one corner to resemble a huge prow of a ship, symbolizing the importance of Hamburg as a sea-port.

Even architects like Gropius and Mies van der Rohe were not untouched by Expressionism. Gropius built a jagged concrete monument to workers killed in the March Rising in 1921, while Mies tried to make expressive use of glass in his skyscraper project for the Friedrichstrasse in Berlin in 1921.

By the early 1920s, though, Expressionism came to seem escapist, and it was quickly superseded by the Neue Sachlichkeit – or New Objectivity.

ABOVE LEFT **'Einstein House', Potsdam, Erich Mendelsohn, 1921**
The plastic quality of the finished Einstein House can be seen in Mendelsohn's highly stylized sketch (left).

OPPOSITE ABOVE **Chilehaus, Hamburg, Fritz Höger, 1923**
Although a minnow by American standards, the 10 storey Chilehaus was one of the first substantial office buildings to be constructed in the centre of a European town.

OPPOSITE BELOW **Eigen Haard Housing, Amsterdam, Michel de Klerk, 1917–20**
No two flats were alike in this development for workers, which combined assorted bulges, towers and other unexpected shapes with imaginative patterns of brickwork.

DE STIJL AND HOLLAND

De Stijl magazine – the title means 'Style' – was founded in 1917. The name comprised a like-minded group of confident – if not arrogant – painters, sculptors and architects who loosely believed in the application of geometric abstraction. Piet Mondrian was one of the earliest to exploit the potential of geometric abstract images that relied on pure colour and form. However, it was notably J J P Oud, Theo van Doesburg and Gerrit Rietveld who translated this idea into three dimensions.

Holland was not directly involved in World War I and, as a consequence, its architects were able to put contemporary ideas on modern architecture into practise well before many other countries. Oud's (1890–1963) design for seaside housing (1917) is an early example of clear, geometric forms, devoid of ornamentation. However, the design is still rigidly symmetrical. Oud, like many of his contemporaries was greatly influenced by H P Berlage, particularly in his 'honest' approach to structure and materials. Oud's housing at the Hook of Holland (1924–7) is so puritanical and uncluttered that it appears almost bland.

In 1923 van Doesburg presented plans and a model for a house which crystallized the De Stijl philosophy, but it was Rietveld's house for Mrs Schroeder (1923–4) that put the theories into practise. Influenced by Wright's use of asymmetrical plans in his Prairie Style houses, the Schroeder house appears to be constructed out of overlapping and intersecting two-dimensional planes that enclose three-dimensional space. The white and grey walls of the exterior are cut and highlighted by the graphic lines of the balcony railings and the window mullions which are painted red, blue, yellow and black. The distribution of wall to window space is approximately equal, so that the solidity of construction is undermined by the sheer volume of openings. Inside, the abstract geometric theme is maintained throughout. By abolishing all the traditional signs by which a building is 'read' and understood – symmetry, a fixed plan, obvious load-bearing supports – Rietveld created a blueprint with seemingly endless possibilities.

Influenced by both the early Dutch Expressionists and the architecture of the De Stijl group, were the architects Willem Dudok (1884–1974) and Johannes Duiker (1890–1935). In Dudok's work, notably the Juliana school at Hilversum (1923) can be seen the reduction to structural essentials and the asymmetricality of Modernist design, but the use of 'warm' materials such as red brick and of deeply pitched roofs are strikingly individualistic. Duiker's commitment to the 'International Style' of the Modern Movement was more profound. His buildings such as the Zonnestraal Sanatorium, Hilversum (1926–8, with Bijvoet) and the Open Air School in Amsterdam (1930–32) with their curtain-wall fenestration and white concrete look to the Bauhaus.

ABOVE **Housing scheme, Hook of Holland, JJP Oud, 1924–27**
This scheme comprised two terraces of cheap housing with shops at the end of each block. The apparent simplicity of the houses with their white-painted rendered façades and horizontal bands of windows looks forward to the full-blown International Style.

LEFT **The Schroeder house, Utrecht, Gerrit Rietveld, 1923–4**
Rietveld used a lightweight steel frame for this house so that the walls were no longer load-bearing. This meant that internal walls could be positioned where desired rather than where necessary. Panels of reinforced concrete were used to create balconies and overhangs.

THE BAUHAUS

The paradox that emerges from the turbulent history of the Bauhaus is that, while founded in a spirit that recognized the supreme importance of 'the building', for the first eight years architecture was not studied in its own right. In spite of this, the influence of the Bauhaus is still seen in the use of mass-produced prefabricated components and in the functional design of much of today's new housing. The Bauhaus also helped change the way architecture is taught – particularly in the United States – by giving students a practical training in arts and crafts and helping to establish Modernism in the syllabus.

The period immediately after World War I was a time of great economic problems in Germany, and it was by coincidence that the city of Weimar, where the Bauhaus was founded in 1919, had just been the seat of the new national convention, giving its name to the 'Weimar Republic'.

To some extent, the seeds of the Bauhaus had been planted before the war by the Werkbund, an association set up in 1907 at the prompting of Hermann Muthesius (1861–1927) with the dual aim of improving the quality of manufactured goods and promoting the role of designers in industry. Among the designers involved in the Werkbund was the Belgian Henrí Van de Velde, who set up a school of arts and crafts in Weimar. This school provided the premises and some of the staff for the Bauhaus.

Walter Gropius (1883–1969), best-known at that time for his Fagus factory at Alfeld-an-der-Leine, was chosen as director from a list supplied by Van de Velde. In his opening proclamation, Gropius urged the breaking down of barriers between artists and craftsmen, at the same time stating unequivocally: 'The ultimate aim of all creative activity is the building'.

The Bauhaus was set up as a series of workshops and in its initial form was inspired by an admiration for Britain's Arts and Crafts movement. Among the initial teachers were such renowned artists as Johannes Itten and Lionel Feininger, later joined by Paul Klee and Wassily Kandinsky.

All students had to take a generalized *Vorkurs*, taught by Itten, which in many ways was a prototype for the foundation course taken by many art students today. The workshops were intended to produce designs that could be sold to industry, but achieved little success in the early years.

Gropius, meanwhile, retained his architectural practice together with his partner Adolf Meyer, and in 1921 they were commissioned to build a villa for the industrialist Adolf Sommerfeld. The Sommerfeld Haus provided the first opportunity for Bauhaus students to become involved in designing for a real building, and they produced the interiors, fittings and furniture. Constructed entirely from wood, it resembled a log cabin in the traditional

Heimatstil, and was adorned with Expressionist wood carvings and stained glass. Expressionism was on the way out in Germany, however, to be replaced by a more rational style known as Neue Sachlichkeit – New Objectivity.

The following year, 1922, the Bauhaus changed direction, turning away from Arts and Crafts towards machines and technology. Itten left and was replaced by the Hungarian Lászlo Moholy-Nagy, while Gropius revised many of his original ideas under the influence of the Dutch Abstract Cubist Theo van Doesburg.

In 1923 the Bauhaus put on its first important exhibition at which the central exhibit was an experimental house designed by the painter Georg Muche. The Haus am Horn was one of the first prototypes for a house that could be made from mass-produced components. Its simple structure consisted of a square frame of steel and concrete with a clerestory-lit central living room surrounded by the other rooms. The prevailing spirit was of functionality, with each room built to fulfil a single purpose, and Marcel Breuer's (1902–81) kitchen was especially prophetic, making use of a continuous work surface with cupboards suspended above and below.

In 1925, growing nationalist hostility forced the Bauhaus to leave Weimar. Gropius found a new location in the industrial city of Dessau, where sufficient financial support was provided to construct a complex of buildings to house the school. The Bauhaus at Dessau consisted of two blocks linked by an enclosed bridge, housing lecture rooms, workshops, student accommodation, a refectory, a theatre, a gymnasium and Gropius and Meyer's architectural practice. The skeleton was of reinforced concrete, while one side of the workshops consisted of a glass curtain wall, and the roof was flat, covered by a new waterproof material. Like the Haus am Horn, the new buildings were striking by their adherence to functionality and by the absence of decoration. Gropius also built a series of houses for himself and the teaching staff on a nearby avenue, based on plans he had drawn up for a projected housing estate in Weimar.

At Dessau, the Bauhaus entered a mature, post-experimentation phase, geared towards the training of industrial designers and the production of designs that were first of all practical. Marcel Breuer produced his famous chairs of bent tubular steel, plated in chrome, upholstered in leather.

The architecture department was set up in 1927 under the Swiss-born Hannes Meyer (1889–1954), and one of its first commissions was to assist Gropius with an experimental housing project in Dessau's Törten district. It was the first chance for Gropius to put his theories on building from standardized components to the test on a large scale. Each house took three days to construct, with components such as concrete wall panels being made on site. Although three stages of the estate were eventually completed, the techniques were flawed, and within a few years many of the houses suffered from cracks and dampness. The Törten estate was also the site for an all-steel house designed by Muche and Richard Paulick, who treated its steel skin as a feature instead of trying to hide it.

Gropius left the Bauhaus in 1928 to concentrate on his own practice and was succeeded by Hannes Meyer, who immediately set the Bauhaus on a new course of social responsibility. Eclectic tastes were dropped in favour of design for the masses, with the intention of producing inexpensive items such as plywood furniture that could be afforded by working people.

Under Meyer, the Bauhaus thrived economically, but growing political pressures forced his resignation after just two years. Mies van der Rohe (1886–1969), already an accomplished technician in steel and glass, took over. He introduced a greater emphasis on architectural theory, and concentrated once more on

OPPOSITE **Fagus Works, Alfeld-an-der-Leine, Walter Gropius, 1911**
One of the first truly modern buildings, the Fagus Works was essentially a cubic block incorporating glass curtain-walling that extended around the corners with no need for additional support.

RIGHT **Model Factory and Office Building, Walter Gropius, 1914**
This building, constructed for the Werkbund Exhibition in Cologne, was just as striking in its modernity as the Fagus factory.

producing exclusive designs for a wealthy élite. Despite Mies' attempts to keep politics out of the Bauhaus, it was closed by the government in 1932 and the buildings were ransacked by the Nazis. A final attempt to revive the Bauhaus in a disused Berlin factory came to an abrupt end when it was raided by police and the Bauhaus was closed for good.

In the following years, Gropius, Mies van der Rohe, Moholy-Nagy and Breuer were among those who joined the exodus of artists and intellectuals from Nazi Germany to the United States. There, they achieved influential positions and disseminated the ideas of the Bauhaus, with Moholy-Nagy even going so far as to create a 'New Bauhaus' in Chicago in 1937. Mies van der Rohe became Dean of Architecture at the Illinois Institute of Technology, while Gropius took the Chair of Architecture at Harvard, and both were instrumental in ensuring the long-overdue acceptance of Modernism by the American establishment.

ABOVE **Workshops, Bauhaus at Dessau, Walter Gropius, 1925–6**
Here the curtain-wall is at last fully developed, and forms a transparent screen, completely exposing the structure within.

RIGHT **Siemensstadt Housing, Berlin, Walter Gropius, 1929–30**
The third in a series of housing projects Gropius undertook after leaving the Bauhaus, Simensstadt was a development of low-cost flats fitted with modern conveniences, constructed with the techniques of prefabrication Gropius had pioneered at Dessau.

OPPOSITE **Students hostel, Bauhaus at Dessau, Walter Gropius, 1925–26**
As well as being connected to the teaching areas at the Bauhaus, the rooms in the hostel were individually served from the kitchen by a system of hatches and food lifts.

BELOW **Zuyev Workers' Club, Moscow, I Golosov, 1927–8**
The giant cylinder of glass is balanced on the right-hand side of the façade by a more solid composition.

ABOVE **Rusakov Workers' Club, Moscow, Konstantin Melnikov, 1927–8**
The giant projections which overhang the façade of this building contain the uppermost seats of the auditorium. The arrangement of sculptural volumes reflects an interest in contemporary Constructivist abstract painting.

OPPOSITE **Reconstruction of the Monument to the Third International, VE Tatlin, 1920**
The original scheme envisaged by Tatlin comprised a 990-ft (300-m) high steel frame from which hung the glass assembly rooms. Not surprisingly, the scheme was more a vehicle of political propaganda than a practical building project.

RUSSIA AND CONSTRUCTIVISM

The 1917 Revolution in Russia not only did away with existing political and social structures, and abolished private property (1918), it also brought with it a new regime that put existing styles of architecture under review. Such political upheaval inevitably cried out for utopian solutions and artists and architects in attempting to find suitable expressions looked to abstraction, mechanization and the work of the Constructivists in particular.

Vladimir Tatlin's (1885–1953) project for a Monument to the Third International (1920) presented one dynamic scheme to house the congress halls of state. The halls were contained within a cube, a pyramid and a cylinder (all revolving) which were suspended inside a giant spiral nearly 990ft (300m) high. The project may have been fantastic and embedded in political ideology rather than reality, but it does reveal a fundamentally 'free' interpretation of architecture more allied to machines and fairground structures than to classic styles.

Equally fantastic was the design for Lenin's Tribune devised by El Lissitzky (1890–1941) in the early 1920s. However, such structures as Tatlin's and Lissitzky's were theoretical rather than practical and, not surprisingly, the little architecture that was built during the early 1920s was still fundamentally conservative. Other designs, less fantastic but not built, were those of the Vesnin brothers for the Palace of Labour (1923) and the Pravda Building (1924), both in Moscow. The buildings are comprised of geometric blocks, rigidly gridded on the exterior, but lightened with aerials and wires to suggest enormous radio sets.

Proof that avant-garde ideas had begun to permeate the country came with Konstantin Melnikov's design of the Soviet Union's pavilion at the 1925 Exposition des Arts Décoratifs. Melnikov (1890–1974) was a member of the Association of New Architects (ASNOVA) and his pavilion was certainly a bold statement amongst the largely Art Deco pavilions of the exhibition. Melnikov's work, appropriately enough, was inspired by factory buildings, with its vast expanses of glass and girder-like construction. In keeping with the beliefs of ASNOVA, Melnikov believed that architecture was a vital tool for post-Revolution Russia and its forms should somehow support and establish the system.

Not all Russian architects were of like mind. The Association of Contemporary Architects (OCA), of which Moisei Ginzberg and the Vesnin brothers were members, criticized such idealistic doctrine for not emphasizing more practical considerations. It concerned itself with addressing the basic problem of how best to house families, particularly in communal projects. The Narkomfin apartments designed by Ginzberg and I Milinis (1928) showed one solution based firmly on Le Corbusier's work – the body of the building was lifted off the ground on thin columns.

ABOVE **The Villa Savoye, Poissy, near Paris, Le Corbusier, 1928–9**
This villa displayed Le Corbusier's 'Five Points of a New Architecture' – a roof terrace, *pilotis*, a free plan, strip windows and a free composition of the facade.

LE CORBUSIER

The architect most responsible for formalizing international Modernism was Charles-Edouard Jeanneret (or Le Corbusier, a pseudonym he adopted from 1920 onwards). As a young architect Le Corbusier (1887–1965) was fortunate enough to work in the offices of both Auguste Perret and Peter Behrens. From the former he was able to comprehend the possibilities of reinforced concrete; from the latter he was able to learn the positive implications of combining design with large-scale mechanization. Both themes came together in his Dom-ino housing scheme (1914–15) with which he hoped to provide quick, cheap dwellings. Designed as a kit, each unit consisted of a six-pillared reinforced concrete frame which supported cantilevered slabs of reinforced concrete. The 'bare bones' design based on strict geometric principles and flexible in the manner in which the building could be sub-divided, highlighted his preoccupation with creating a new basic system of construction. The walls no longer carried any weight so that they could be placed anywhere.

Together with his friend Amédée Ozenfant (1886–1966), Le Corbusier began painting, creating what they dubbed 'After Cubism' paintings, but in which one still discerns the Classical values of harmony and balance (including the golden section). In 1920 he and Ozenfant set up a magazine entitled *L'Esprit Nouveau* which underlined the need for a new architecture in tune with the developments of the machine age. While Le Corbusier was uninspired by buildings of the immediate past, he certainly admired architecture of Classical antiquity and believed wholeheartedly in the notion that there existed inherent forms of beauty. A selection of articles taken from the magazine were

BELOW & PAGE 52 **The Villa Savoye, Poissy, near Paris, Le Corbusier, 1928–9**
Le Corbusier deliberately undermined the 'reading' of separate internal and external spaces by creating large picture windows which fell to the floor and ramps and staircases that were easily 'at home' either within the house or on the terrace outside.

published in book form under the title *Vers une architecture* (1923), which proved to be one of the most significant architectural publications of the 20th century.

Le Corbusier's sketches for the Maison Citrohan (1919–22) reveals the hallmarks of his own style – a geometric white block constructed out of concrete, raised on slender columns (*pilotis*), a flat roof, and lots of windows set flush with the wall and terraces. Each element of the house has been reduced to its bare functional essentials, geometrically expressed – thus it has become (in Le Corbusier's much-quoted phrase) a 'machine for living in'.

Le Corbusier's plans for a large city, *The Contemporary City for Three Million Inhabitants*, which was exhibited at the Salon d'Automne in 1922, revealed his utopian ideals: a frighteningly totalitarian approach to providing standardized, uniform housing, much of it in high-rise blocks. His vision was total, from small-scale considerations like cupboards and lighting to the concept of housing entire cities. An apartment from a similar scheme provided the basis for the *L'Esprit Nouveau* pavilion at the 1925 Exposition des Arts Décoratifs in Paris. Amid the otherwise

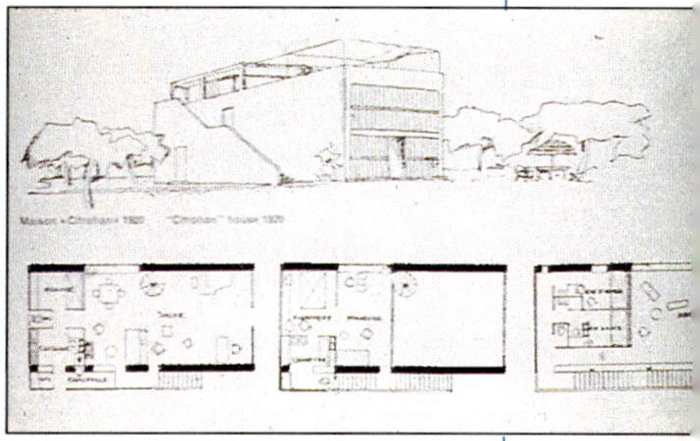

ABOVE **Design for the Maison Citrohan, Le Corbusier, 1919–22**
Le Corbusier's fascination with machines in general and cars in particular was such that the name of this important early scheme was based on that of a well-known carmaker's name. Cars featured in *Vers une architecture* next to Classical Greek architecture.

ABOVE (***see*** **page 51**)

traditional stands, the pavilion must have appeared stark.

The Villa Savoye at Poissy (1928–9) neatly summarizes Le Corbusier's self-proclaimed 'Five Points of a New Architecture' – a free plan, a free façade, *pilotis*, a terrace and ribbon windows. While appearing to implement his machine-inspired ideas, it also reveals a sculptural treatment of forms, an element of his work that became more pronounced as he grew older.

Having established his reputation with a number of domestic commissions, climaxing in the apotheosis of his beliefs – the Villa Savoye – Le Corbusier turned his attentions to large-scale projects, not least of which was his plans for the Ville Radieuse ('Shining City'). He also submitted a number of plans for competitions including those for the Palace of the League of Nations (1927) and for the Palace of the Soviets (1931). The latter included an enormous assembly hall with a roof suspended from a giant

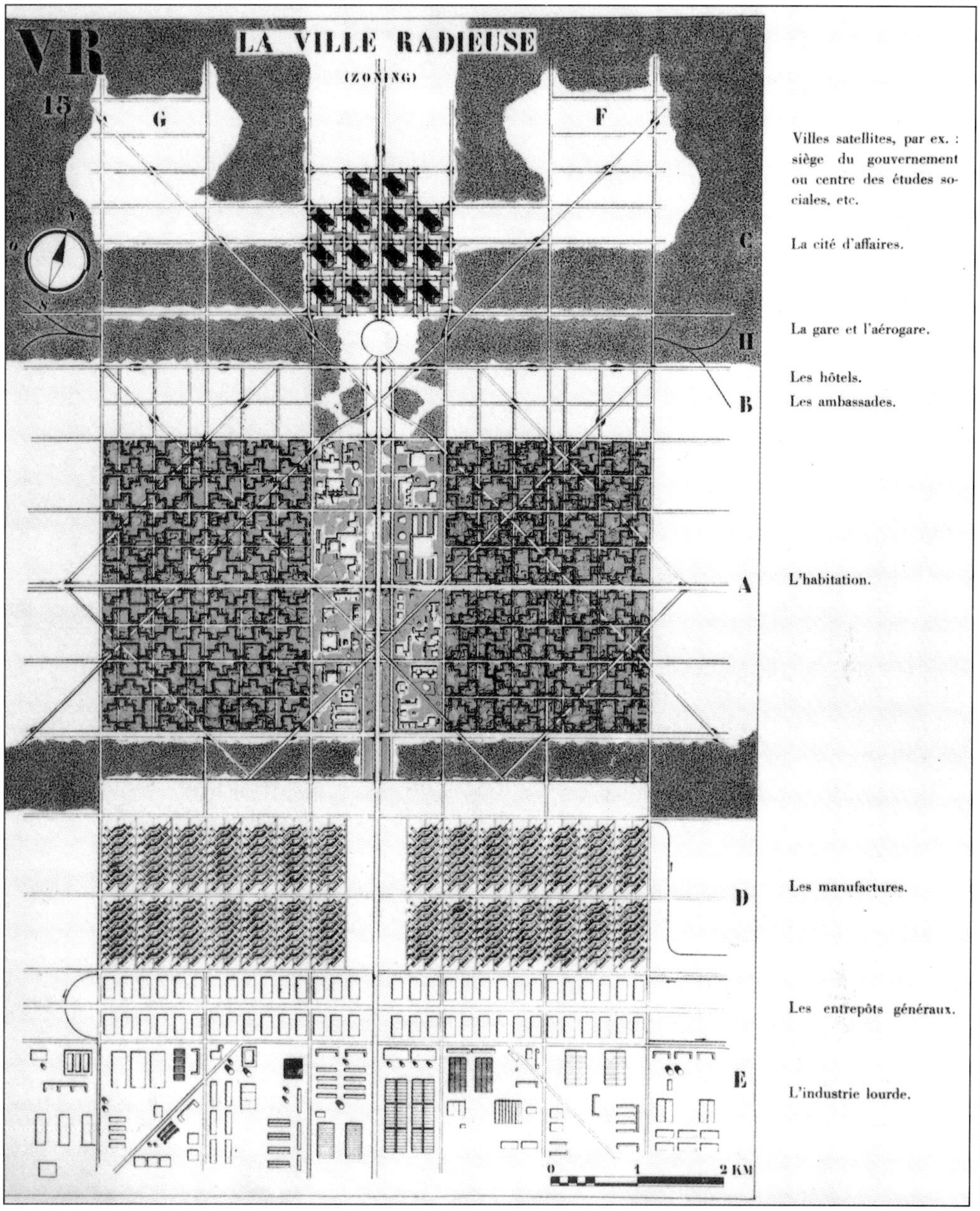

parabolic arch. Successful projects included the Maison de Refuge, Paris (1930–3), a large building with a ship-like presence, one wall of which was almost entirely glass. The Swiss pavilion (1930–1) which Le Corbusier designed for the Cité Universitaire in Paris marks a shift in emphasis towards a more organic treatment of concrete. Like the Villa Savoye, the main body of the building is suspended above ground by means of supports. In place of the slender white *pilotis* are curved, robust bare-concrete pillars. The 'cells' of the student rooms within are expressed on the facade to form a grid. The stairs and lift have been encased within a secondary curvilinear support block. This treatment, whereby the volumes within dictate the exterior, proved to be a much quoted model during the 1950s and 1960s.

ABOVE **La Ville Radieuse, Le Corbusier, 1935**
Le Corbusier designed a number of total plans for towns and cities, such as this symmetrical scheme, in which rows of identical skyscrapers were positioned on geometric grids. Utopian in scale and intention, these totalitarian schemes were not surprisingly never built.

MIES VAN DER ROHE AND FUNCTIONALISM

The Modernist architecture built in the 1950s and 1960s can be separated, in a very general sense, into two camps – that which looked to the more 'sculptural' concrete architecture of Le Corbusier and that which looked to the 'steel and glass' architecture of Mies van der Rohe.

The design submitted to the Berlin Friedrichstrasse Skyscraper competition of 1921 was the crystallization of this Mies van der Rohe style. The building consisted of no more than an immense steel-frame, sheathed in glass. Like the schemes of Tony Garnier and Le Corbusier, the building represented some kind of utopian solution: as if such purity was the necessary conclusion of Functionalism.

Mies van der Rohe's choice of materials was expected, given that his father ran a stonemason's office in which he himself had actually worked. Having worked for Peter Behrens (like Le Corbusier), Mies van der Rohe's early influences included the work of Karl-Friedrich Schinkel, the creator of 19th-century neo-Classical Berlin, and Berlage. His plans for an office block of 1922 utilizes glass to divide the building into vast horizontal slabs; the building is supported 'internally' by piers and cantilevered trays. Unconventionally, the building increases in size gradually with each floor.

In 1923 Mies van der Rohe helped found the Berlin 'G' group which set out its aim as truth to construction and function. In the same year he drew up designs for a brick villa. The plan resembles an abstract graphic pattern akin to the creations of both El Lissitzky and van Doesburg. With a system of overlapping planes, the building also harks back to Frank Lloyd Wright's early work.

In 1927 the Werkbund held a housing exhibition at Stuttgart which was overseen by Mies van der Rohe, and contributors included the rarified group of Gropius, Taut, Le Corbusier, J J P Oud and Mart Stam. Such a gathering obviously testified to the common ground which these architects shared. Mies van der Rohe had the task of designing a site plan that could show off various designs actually built. His solution was an abstract-inspired system of blocks with his own exhibit for an apartment block constituting the focal point.

Functionalism preoccupied some architects more than others. Johannes Brinckmann and Leendert van der Vlugt together with Mart Stam designed and built a factory for the firm of Van Nelle (1927–30) in which practical considerations – light, air, open floor space – dictated the form. Windows from floor to ceiling ran the length of the main building and glazed bridges acted as communi-

ABOVE **1986 reconstruction of the German pavilion, Barcelona, Spain, Ludwig Mies van der Rohe, 1928–9**
Like Rietveld's Schroeder House, this pavilion, built for the 1929 Barcelona Exhibition, comprised a series of planes at angles to each other. The vertical panels of travertine and glass were capped by the slab of the roof, and two pools acted as reflectors.

LEFT **The Farnsworth house, Ludwig Mies van der Rohe, Plano, Illinois, USA, 1945–51** This house is one of the punctation points of 20th-century architecture – with the abolition of external walls in favour of plate-glass windows, the 'barriers' between the exterior and the interior of the house have all but disappeared. Philip Johnson designed a similar 'glass' house at the same time in New Canaan, Connecticut.

BELOW **Van Nelle factory, Rotterdam, Holland, Johannes Brinkmann & Leendert van der Vlugt in association with Mart Stam, 1927–30** Nowhere was glass-curtain Functionalism more appropriate or more successful than for factories, as here at the Van Nelle headquarters. A series of glass-encased walkways linked the buildings and the circular viewing room at the top of the factory housed the factory canteen.

cation links. Such functionalism coupled with the social implications of creating a decent working space undoubtedly dictated a form that was not a 'style' as such (that is, not until later architects began to define it).

R Buckminster Fuller was a Functionalist above all else who dismissed the International Style as unscientific and superficial. His Dymaxion House of the late 1920s presented what he believed to be a truly functional living unit that utilized modern technology to the full. Designed in aluminium, the house was suspended from a central mast which carried all the mechanical services. Like many innovative schemes, the building never presented workable applications.

In 1929 Mies van der Rohe was given the task of designing the German pavilion for the Barcelona exhibition of 1929. Created as a temporary showcase for German design, the pavilion was, in construction terms, a brilliant exercise employing eight narrow steel supports to carry a thin slab which made up the roof. Like the *L'Esprit Nouveau* pavilion by Le Corbusier of four years earlier, this pavilion represented a brilliantly polarized architectural standpoint, a précis of Mies's design ideas.

MODERN MOVEMENTS IN BRITAIN AND SCANDINAVIA

Britain

Throughout the 1920s most large-scale architecture in Britain remained traditional, typified by Reginald Blomfield's brand of French academic Beaux-Arts/Baroque Classicism, such as that which he had used earlier in the century for the scheme for Regent Street. Lutyens too, employed a heavy Classicism for corporate commissions such as the Midland Bank (1924–1939) whereas architects such as Charles Holden, working primarily for the London Passenger Transport Board, allowed the more avant-garde ideas from abroad to permeate their work. From the mid-1920s onwards Art Deco began to be used primarily for commercial buildings. For country houses, a form of neo-Georgian architecture was unchallenging and popular. Some architects could turn their hand to any number of styles depending on the client's wishes: Oliver Hill was equally capable of designing a house in the Classical style as in the International Style.

BELOW **Arnos Grove Underground station, London, C Percy Adams, Charles Holden and JL Pearson, 1922**
The London Underground architects designed buildings that managed to cross the border between Art Deco and early Modernism.

LEFT **Tuberculosis Sanatorium, Paimio, Finland, Alvar Aalto, 1929–33**
Ship-like in presence, the sanatorium consisted of three large blocks linked by a smaller communications block. It was one of the few really large buildings of the early International Style.

OPPOSITE **Penguin Pool, London Zoo, Tecton, 1933**
This sculptural creation was designed by Tecton, an architectural practice that was founded in 1932 by Berthold Lubetkin in association with Anthony Chitty, Lindsey Drake, Michael Dugdale, Valentine Harding, Godfrey Samuel and Frances Skinner. The group is best known for its fantastic creations for London Zoo and for the Highpoint flats in Highgate, north London.

The architect Frederick Etchells translated Le Corbusier's *Vers une architecture* into English and in 1929 designed the Crawford's advertising building which together with Amyas Connell's Ashmole house in Amersham, Buckinghamshire, of a year later, were concrete pieces of evidence that 'Modernism' had arrived.

Its leading exponent in Britain was Berthold Lubetkin. Brought up in Russia and having worked in Perret's office in Paris, Lubetkin was already familiar with Modernist notions before he emigrated to Britain in 1930. There he formed Tecton, a group of like-minded architects, and one of their earliest commissions, in association with the Danish-born engineer Ove Arup, was to build the penguin pool at London Zoo (1933). With its self-supporting embracing ramps of reinforced concrete, the pool falls between architecture and sculpture, looking as much to Constructivist art as to Le Corbusier. The group was commissioned to design a block of flats, Highpoint I (1933–5), in Highgate, north London. The block stands on top of a hill and the large windows and balconies made ample use of the sweeping views. Lubetkin's absorption of Le Corbusier's 'five points' of the new architecture is obvious, with *pilotis* carrying the main body of the building, and a large roof terrace.

Other architects who emigrated to Britain or passed through on the way to the United States included Gropius (who set up in practice with Maxwell Fry), Breuer (who set up in practice with F R S Yorke) and Mendelsohn. The latter was in partnership with Serge Chermayeff and they designed amongst other buildings the De La Warr pavilion in Bexhill, Sussex, a decidedly bold scheme for the countryside. Other architects who produced their own brand of the International Style in the 1930s were Joseph Emberton, the firm of Connell, Ward and Lucas, and Wells Coates (the architect of the Lawn Road Flats of 1934).

Most of these architects were in sympathy with Le Corbusier's brand of Modernism. 'Glass and steel' Modernism, however, also had its supporters. Owen Williams's magnificent factory for Boots the Chemist in Beeston, Nottinghamshire (1930–32) used floor-to-ceiling glass windows that ran the length of the building – like the Van Nelle factory in Rotterdam by Brinckmann, Van der Vlugt and Mart Stam, which had been completed in the previous year. Slater, Moberly, Reilly and Crabtree's curving Peter Jones department store (1936) in Chelsea, London, also used glass curtain-walls on a frame of reinforced concrete.

Scandinavia

Modernism, with its 'hard' materials of concrete, steel and glass, might not appear to be a feasible style in Scandinavia where an appreciation of natural materials prevailed. In fact, Scandinavian architects diluted Modernism with wood and other 'organic' materials to create a peculiarily humane brand of Modernism.

P V Jensen-Klint's Grundtvig church on the outskirts of Copenhagen (1913–22) was a soaring edifice of traditional forms and materials, but it betrayed distinct 'modern' elements, notably its monumentality. Similarly, Gunnar Asplund's design for the Stockholm Public Library (1920–28) reveals a pared-down Classicism which recalls the designs of the 18th-century visionary architect Claude-Nicolas Ledoux.

In 1931 Asplund designed the Stockholm Exhibition buildings which were in the new style. It was, however, Alvar Aalto (1898–1976) of Finland who was the leading exponent of Modernist ideas in Scandinavia in the 1930s. His commission to design the Paimio Sanatorium (1929–33) provided Aalto with the opportunity to employ the new style for a fundamentally humanitarian function where the inherently clinical aspects of the style were entirely appropriate. The sanitorium comprised three main blocks linked by a corridor and a communications block which housed the entrance. The patients' rooms were grouped within a long six-floored block with continuous window-bands providing strong horizontal, ground-hugging lines.

Ship-like in stature, the building seemed to justify modern architecture and at the 1933 CIAM meeting Aalto was congratulated by the 'giants' – Le Corbusier, Gropius and Mies van der Rohe. On a smaller scale, Aalto designed the Villa Mairea in 1938 in which he used wood, stone and brick, as well as turf to cover the roof. This seemingly diverse combination of vernacular and international academicism did, in fact, provide a very real direction for Modernism to take. Similarly, the spectacularly sited, majestic crematorium at Enskede, Stockholm (1939–40) by Asplund, with its minimalist, classically inspired portico, provided a route for future architects working in the Modernist style.

FRANK LLOYD WRIGHT AND AMERICAN PROGRESSIVE ARCHITECTURE

While Europe in the 1920s was charged with new ideas emanating from a small group of intellectual architects, Frank Lloyd Wright (to whom many of them had looked) went through troubled times. Several members of his family were killed when his home, Taliesen, was burned to the ground in 1914. Wright sought solace in Tokyo where he designed the spectacular Imperial Hotel. When he returned, he preoccupied himself with house commissions, many in California. These houses reveal not only the influence of pre-Columbian architecture in Central and South America, but also the consideration that Wright gave to climatic considerations. The Millard house of 1921–3 in Pasadena, California, has a peculiarly decorative finish which lightens the otherwise severe raw concrete of its construction, without interfering with the organic nature of the house.

It was during this period that Rudolf Schindler (1887–1953), an Austrian who left Vienna in 1914, worked in Wright's office before setting up on his own. In 1925–6 he designed the Lovell house at Newport Beach, California, a robust building lifted off the ground by means of solid pillars and bearing the hallmarks of the International Style – white painted concrete, a flat roof, great expanses of glass, and terraces – in tandem with the 'vernacular' Functionalism of Irving Gill. Richard Neutra was another Austrian who had worked with Schindler, producing pieces of hybrid international and local style.

The Philadelphia Savings Fund Society building (1926–31)

BELOW **Johnson Wax Building, Racine, Wisconsin, 1935–50**
Apart from the laboratory tower, the main buildings of this complex are without windows on their exterior walls, being lit by top skylights and internal courts. The tower, one of the last elements to be built, harks back to the streamlining of the 1930s and looks forward to the 'smooth' designs of the 1960s. Giant mushroom-shaped freestanding supports (BELOW LEFT) help break up the vast internal space of this administrative office space. Wright was also responsible for the design of the desks and chairs.

RIGHT **Kaufmann house, Bear Run, Pennsylvania, Frank Lloyd Wright, 1935–9**
Popularly known as Falling Water, this house successfully combined a sensitivity to the landscape with an interest in abstract forms. Vertical sections of the house are made from stone whereas horizontal elements are constructed out of reinforced concrete.

designed by George Howe and William Lescaze is an early attempt to reconcile the building of a skyscraper with the principles of the International Style. The solution which they adopted, involving the use of a podium from which the tower rose, proved to be an often repeated model. It facilitated strong horizontals (so important to the style) at ground level without disturbing the powerful verticality of the building.

In 1932, the Museum of Modern Art in New York housed an exhibition devoted to modern architecture organized by Alfred Barr, Henry-Russell Hitchcock and Philip Johnson which attempted to put the International Style on a more solid footing. However, mainstream American architecture remained largely traditional in flavour with the exception of Art Deco and Art Moderne.

In the 1930s Wright's personal and financial situation stabilized and he produced both small and large-scale commissions including the much publicized Falling Water at Bear Run, Pennsylvania, and the Johnson Wax Building at Racine, Wisconsin. Falling Water (1935) was the product of a relatively unrestricted commission and took Wright's more organic tendencies to extremes with its rock-like projections. The Johnson Wax Building, begun in the same year, looked by contrast almost Art Moderne with its streamlined tower block of internal mushroom-like supports.

ABOVE **Millard house, Pasadena, California, Frank Lloyd Wright, 1921–3**
Popularly known as 'La Miniatura', this house typifies the group of houses that Wright designed in Pasadena at this time. The blocks of solid and perforated prefabricated concrete allowed for climbing plants.

DAILY EXPRESS
SUNDAY EXPRESS
ALL ENQUIRIES TO RECEPTION DESK

ART DECO AND ART MODERNE

The term 'Art Deco' was popularized in the 1960s and is used to describe a largely decorative style (roughly 1920–1940) which is characterized by strong geometric forms, striking colours and graphic sharpness. Named after the Paris Exposition Internationale des Arts Décoratifs et Industriels Modernes (1925), it was this exhibition that provided the first large-scale showcase of the decorative arts and architecture in a 'moderne' style.

It can be argued that Art Moderne was purely the commercial interpretation of Modernism; the two movements certainly shared common influences such as Cubist, Abstract and Expressionist art, the architecture of the Arts and Crafts practitioners, Frank Lloyd Wright and the Secessionists. The Kärntner Bar in Vienna, designed by Adolf Loos in 1907, appears to foresee both Modernism and Art Moderne. Similarly, Le Corbusier's *L'Esprit Nouveau* pavilion at the Exposition was an inspiration to all manner of architects. While Art Moderne and Art Deco were decorative, Modernism was exclusive and rarified, and above all, hard on eyes accustomed to more ornamental and traditional forms of architecture. Art Deco, on the other hand, combined

OPPOSITE **Daily Express Building, London, Sir Owen Williams, 1935–7**
This view of the main entrance hall reveals Williams at his most decorative. Such extremes of ornament were unusual in Britain; this hall might look more at home in either France or America.

BELOW & BOTTOM **Hoover factory, Perivale, London, Wallis Gilbert and Partners, 1932–8**
Egyptian influences are easily discernible in this spectacular palace of industry.

the solid geometric shapes thought of at the time as decidedly 'modern', but was mellowed with sculptural ornament, metalwork and colour.

The Exposition highlighted Paris as the centre of the Art Deco style. The grand Art Deco entrance to the Exposition, the 'Porte d'Honneur', with extensive decorative metalwork by Edgar Brandt, blatantly announced it to the world. Within, Robert Mallet-Steven's 'Pavillon du Tourisme' personified the more Modernist tendencies of Art Moderne whereas the furniture designer's Emile-Jacques Ruhlmann's 'Hôtel d'un Collectionneur', designed by the architect Pierre Patout, displayed a more restrained Classical form of Art Deco. However, the Exposition by its very nature was not only international – pavilions representing many countries betrayed 'modern' sentiments – but also temporary.

In the years following the Exposition, commercial Art Moderne, or Art Deco, appeared throughout Europe and the United States. In France itself, Art Deco is distinct for its restrained reductivist façades, lightened with floral and figurative ironwork and sculpture. In Britain the two styles were used frequently for the many hundreds of cinemas that were sprouting up throughout the country; the façade of the Leicester Square Odeon in London is a particularly fine example of Art Moderne and is sheathed in shiny black cladding. London Underground, which underwent an extensive expansion in the 1920s and 1930s, built many stations in a much more understated Modernist Art Moderne.

The country in which Art Deco and Moderne architecture really blossomed was the United States. Generously fed on the

home-grown Modernist ideas of Frank Lloyd Wright, and eager to employ styles of architecture devoid of overt historical and cultural associations, the United States took to Art Deco enthusiastically. The style was adopted not only for large-scale structures such as New York skyscrapers and Miami Beach apartment blocks, but also small buildings such as diners. Often clad in a skin of stainless steel, American diners embody the impact of 'streamlining' (the adulation of machine and car technology and styling), an important element of Art Deco style.

Skyscrapers, such as the Chrysler Building by William van Alen (1928–30), were the pinnacle of Art Deco achievement. A soaring testament to corporate acceptance, these skyscrapers dominated Manhattan architecture in particular during the late 1920s and through the 1930s, and they included the Chanin Building (Sloan & Robertson, 1929), the Empire State Building (Shreve, Lamb & Harmon, 1930–1), the McGraw-Hill Building (Raymond Hood, 1930–1) and the Rockefeller Center (Raymond Hood and others, 1931–9).

OPPOSITE ABOVE **Apartment block, Ealing, London, 1930s**
Muted Art Moderne was often used for the vast quantity of speculative building that went up in Britain between the wars. Green roof tiles are peculiar to this period of architecture and were sometimes adopted for 'Spanish hacienda' style housing.

OPPOSITE BELOW **Elevator doors, Chrysler Building, New York, William van Alen, 1928–30**
Inlaid with veneers of wood and brass, these doors are sumptuous examples of full-blown American Art Deco.

RIGHT **Olympia exhibition halls, London, Joseph Emberton, 1929–30**
Monumental in scale and appearance, these exhibition halls were expressive examples of the combination of Art Deco and Modernist ideals – Art Moderne.

LEFT **Empire State Building, New York, Shreve, Lamb and Harmon, 1930–1**
For many years the tallest building in the world, the Empire State Building rises 102 storeys above the Manhattan skyline.

OPPOSITE LEFT **Chrysler Building, New York, William van Alen, 1928–30**
Like many of the skyscrapers being built in Manhattan at this time, the Chrysler Building was a vertical 'city' of offices with its many elevators serving as the main routes of communication.

OPPOSITE RIGHT **Rockefeller Center, New York, Raymond Hood and others, 1931–9**
This massive development occupied several blocks of mid-town Manhattan. As well as several soaring skyscrapers, it included Radio City Music Hall (interior design by Donald Deskey), a vast underground network of shops and restaurants and an ice rink.

STATE ARCHITECTURE

The rising tide of nationalism in the period between the two World Wars produced calls in various countries for an architecture fit to represent the state. In some cases the call came from newly-formed nations, such as Finland, eager to assert an identity to the rest of the world. In others the motive was to monumentalize ideological or imperial dreams such as Nazi Germany's Thousand-year Reich or the British Empire.

In general, Modernism was rejected as unsuitable for such purposes, and the style adopted was usually a revamped version of Ancient Greece or Rome, in varying degrees of banality. Modernism's failing, in nationalist eyes, was its concern with functionality and with the needs of the people who would occupy

ABOVE **Drawing for the Palace of the Soviets, Moscow, IS Iofan, 1937**
Looking like a cross between a Roman temple and a skyscraper, Iofan's extravagant plan underwent numerous revisions, including the replacement of the huge figure of Lenin by that of a 'worker', before building eventually began.

LEFT **Haus der Kunst, Munich, Paul Ludwig Troost, 1933–7**
Troost deployed a sterile version of the Tuscan order in a bid to rebuild Munich as the capital of National Socialism.

RIGHT **The Viceroy's House, New Delhi, Edwin Lutyens, 1913–29**
The most monumental of all the buildings in New Delhi, in spite of its obvious Classical influence the Viceroy's House betrays a flavour of India.

buildings. Its abstract, often austere forms were not deemed capable of conveying the sense of power and permanence required to represent an empire or nation.

Under Hitler and Stalin, Modernist movements such as those of the Bauhaus and the Constructivists were actively suppressed. The choice of a classical model was in many ways an anti-intellectual, regressive tendency. Classicism in the early 20th century was not, however, the exclusive language of totalitarian regimes.

In Scandinavia, Hack Kampmann's elegantly colonnaded police headquarters in Copenhagen, completed in 1924, was one of a series of buildings that provided evidence of a persistent Classical feeling. The City Library in Stockholm four years later, by Gunnar Asplund, and J S Sirén's 1926 Parliament Building in Helsinki, were characteristic of a simplified or 'cut-down' Classicism which sometimes accommodated some Modernist features. In Asplund's building, for example, the domed roof originally envisaged was replaced by a flat-roofed cylindrical drum.

In the early years of the 20th century, Edwin Lutyens became a convert to Classicism, which he took up in preference to the Arts and Crafts style of his previous country houses. In 1913, Lutyens (together with Herbert Baker) was commissioned to build a new capital city for India at Delhi.

New Delhi was an attempt by the British to reassert their grip on an India that increasingly aspired to home rule. The government hoped that by reviving some of the tradition of the Moghul court around the 'King-Emperor' George V in a new monumental capital of the Raj, calls for self-rule might be defeated. This hope proved over-optimistic, as independence was granted to India just 15 years after New Delhi was completed in 1931.

The challenge of New Delhi was to incorporate both Moghul and Western Classical themes. On the first count, Lutyens and Baker largely failed, although there is an exotic flavour to the detailing and dome of Lutyen's Viceroy's House, the grandest and most dignified of all the buildings in New Delhi (now the residence of the President of India).

More significant as an indicator of the way the tide was turning

ABOVE **A Hitler youth hostel, c1940**
The tradition of German medieval houses – *heimatstil* – was deployed by Hitler to serve the people.

LEFT **Civiltà Italica, EUR, Rome – Guerrini, La Padula, Romano, 1940**
One of the few buildings to be completed before Mussolini's showcase project, the Exposizione Universale di Roma, was abandoned.

OPPOSITE **Museo della Civiltà Romana, EUR, Rome – Aschieri, Bernardini, Pascoletti and Peressutti, begun 1937**

BELOW LEFT **Zeppelinfeld, Nuremberg, Albert Speer, 1934**
Designed to survive for thousands of years as a ruin, in its brief lifetime Speer's vast parade ground was the setting for Nazi pageantry.

against Modernism was the 1927 competition to design a new headquarters for the League of Nations in Geneva. Although Modernists like Le Corbusier and Hannes Meyer entered, a simplified Classical design was chosen.

Four years later, the confrontation was repeated in Moscow, where Stalin was keen to make his mark by erecting a monumental Palace of the Soviets in the Kremlin. The subsequent competition, with Molotov chairing the judging, attracted entries from Le Corbusier, Gropius and Perret, but a Classical design by the Russian I S Iofan was selected. The construction of Iofan's winning entry began only after several years of revisions. The final plan was a tower consisting of successive colonnaded tiers, surmounted by a preposterous statue of Lenin.

The Palace of the Soviets was abandoned well before completion, but it proved a turning point in Soviet architecture, which lapsed into an endless profusion of sculpturally adorned imitations of Ancient Greece, often incorporating tower-blocks reminiscent of New York's Woolworth building, right down to the ornate interiors of the Moscow Metro, begun in 1934.

In Germany, the Nazi's opposition to Modernism was unequivocal. The Bauhaus was closed down and ransacked soon after

Hitler came to power, while the increasingly popular International Style was spurned as being socialist in intent and too cosmopolitan in its outlook.

Hitler had a strong personal interest in architecture. Ideally, he would have liked to combine traditional German styles with the monumentality of Ancient Rome, but as this was not possible he had to use each for separate purposes. *Heimatstil* – the tradition of small, traditional gabled houses with pitched roofs – was revived for housing, clubs, youth hostels and training centres.

While Functionalism was still tolerated in factories, Classicism became the architecture of the Nazi state. Paul Ludwig Troost was appointed state architect, and he built a group of Renaissance-inspired headquarters buildings for the Nazi party in Munich. He was succeeded by Albert Speer, who designed the vast Zeppelinfeld stadium for the Nuremberg rallies of 1934 onward.

Speer wanted his buildings to stand for 1,000 years, and he used giant blocks of stone like the Ancient Romans, in preference to reinforced concrete or steel. Everything he built was on a massive scale. He started a second stadium, the Deutches Stadion, which would hold 405,000 people when completed. He planned a meeting hall for the centre of Berlin with a dome 820 ft (250 m) wide – three times the size of any other in the world. Speer planned to build a new centre for Berlin based on Imperial Rome, but like most of his plans, it was never realized.

In Italy, Mussolini also wanted to revive the glory of Ancient Rome, but his approach was both more imaginative and more ambivalent. Modernism was adapted to assertive propaganda uses, and, perhaps because of the ideological links between Fascism and the Futurist movement, non-Fascist architects like Pier Luigi Nervi and Giacomo Matté Trucco were able to work unhampered right up to World War II.

However, Classicism was favoured by Mussolini after he assumed total power, and in 1931 he embarked on a plan to open up areas of Rome and expose more of its ancient buildings. He constructed the Via della Conciliazione in front of St Peters, an avenue lined with lamp pylons in the shape of Egyptian obelisks. Mussolini already had a huge obelisk inscribed with his name at the Foro Mussolini, a stadium built in 1927.

In 1932, Mussolini initiated construction of a new university city in Rome, which was led by the architect Marcello Piacentini. The buildings were typically of reinforced concrete frame, and brickwork faced with stone. The most grandiose was Piacentini's Rectorate, fronted by four giant pilasters.

In 1938, Piacentini received an even greater commission: to build a permanent exhibition of the achievements of the Fascist state called the Esposizione Universale di Roma (EUR) at a site three miles south of the city. A large number of monumental buildings were envisaged but few were completed before the war suspended construction in 1940. The main building to be finished was the Civiltà Italica, each façade of which was composed of six rows of arches, described by one critic as 'an ultimate architectural banality'.

1945
1970

INTRODUCTION 1945–1970

Like World War I, World War II drained resources in Europe and building industries were severely restricted. However, unlike the first war, widespread bombing meant that many more European countries witnessed wholesale destruction. The centres of cities and towns such as Dresden in Germany and Coventry in Britain were left with very few structurally sound buildings as the war came to an end in 1945. Such devastation, of course, provided exhaustive building opportunities. Many countries had been crippled financially by the war and it took several years for building programmes to be designed, let alone put into production. In the meantime, many temporary and factory-made dwellings were manufactured and erected to meet the severe housing shortages, including prefabricated and mobile homes.

After the war, new socialist and democratic governments in both Europe and the United States oversaw the development of wide-scale social welfare, promising protection 'from the cradle to the grave' with improved housing, education and health facilities. Such good intentions obviously necessitated massive state building – houses, schools, universities and hospitals were needed, and fast. Local authorities with limited funds at their disposal and large numbers of people to care for seized on Modernism because it was not only a new style of architecture for a new style of government, but it was also fundamentally cheaper to build.

Under such patronage, Modernism thrived throughout the 1950s and 1960s, and developed into two very distinct styles. The first used concrete as a sculptural medium and its sheer strength can be seen when Le Corbusier used it to dramatic effect at Notre Dame du Haut, Ronchamp, France (1950–55). This style of Modernism was generally used for large-scale public buildings (for mainly privately funded works). It could be argued that some of Frank Lloyd Wright's structures of this period, such as the Guggenheim Museum in New York (1943–59), are fundamentally Modernist in approach although he preferred to stay one step removed from European Modernism.

The second style of Modernism relied on steel and glass for a harder, more rigid appearance and its chief exponent, Mies van der Rohe, used the Farnsworth House in Fox River, Illinois (1945–51) as a précis of this form of steel and glass construction. Throughout this period, it was used extensively for office buildings in particular. At the same time, experimental architects such as Buckminster Fuller and Bruce Goff designed buildings in the United States that turned their backs resolutely on the 'four walls and a roof' concept of architecture, producing wonderfully individualist works.

LEFT **Solomon R Guggenheim Museum, New York, Frank Lloyd Wright, 1943–59**
The façade of this building emphasizes the spiral ramp of the gallery within. The mildly irritating fact that one foot is always lower than the other when viewing a picture is negligible beside the sheer drama of the interior space.

OPPOSITE **Unité d'Habitation, Marseilles, Le Corbusier, 1946–52**
Le Corbusier became increasingly occupied with the sculptural properties of concrete. Here, on the roof of this vast housing complex, he was able to give full expression to his theories.

BUILDING FOR THE MASSES

ABOVE The blanket bombing of World War II flattened entire cities creating the acute post-war housing crisis.

World War II resulted in the largest unintentional land clearance scheme the world had ever seen.

Whole cities, such as Dresden and Coventry, were flattened, countless historic buildings were lost – especially due to the Baedeker raids (so named as they used the Baedeker Guide Books to pick out their targets) which aimed to lower public morale by destroying places of no military value but of massive architectural and historical importance and beauty.

Post-war Germany was left with 2.3 million dwellings out of a total of 10.5 totally destroyed and almost half damaged in some way. In France 5% of the 1939 tally of buildings was destroyed, and of the other areas affected by the war it was only the United States and, in Europe, the German-occupied Scandinavian countries which escaped major damage.

This wholesale destruction resulted in an acute housing crisis with soldiers, refugees and ex-prisoners of war returning home to find not houses but rubble.

To add to this turmoil the industrial centres – the ones that remained intact – had given over all their manufacturing capacity

BELOW **La Ville Radieuse, Le Corbusier, 1935**
One of Le Corbusier's town planning studies, this is an early vision of the high-rise buildings to come.

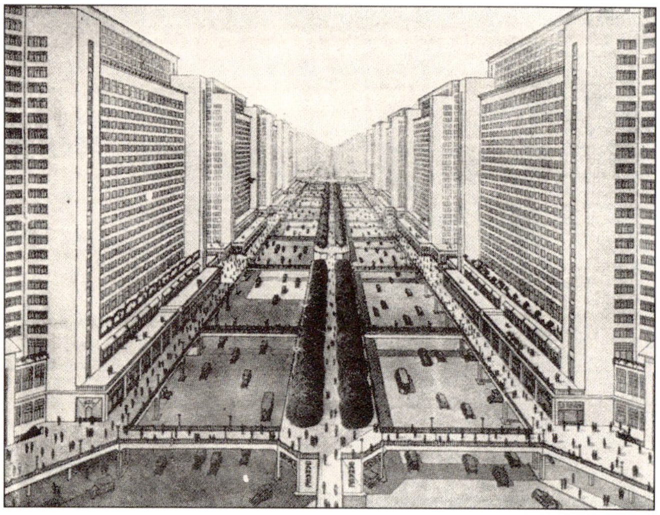

to the war effort so were not geared up to providing peace-time commodities. Yet people firmly believed that they could build a brave new world from the ruins left by the war and the American Marshall Plan in 1947, with its aim of supporting economic reconstruction, was instrumental in putting Western Europe back on the road to recovery.

The destruction offered social and architectural opportunities never seen before. Unfortunately, governments were so desperate to rebuild quickly that many opportunities were wasted and minimum-standard housing, haphazardly sited, became the reality, rather than well-thought-out schemes providing quality housing that would have taken longer to realize yet would have been better in the long term.

In the United States, this rush to build resulted in vast stretches of prefabricated 'tract' housing, such as Levittown on Long Island – a 17,500 house development by William Levitt, who pioneered the mass-produced assembly-line approach to house building called 'site fabrication', which was so fast that 35 houses a day could be constructed.

These cheap and easy to build prefab houses went someway towards fulfilling the American dream of a home for everyone. A dream also helped along by large federal loans to potential purchasers. But unfortunately these homes came in only four or five basic styles – ranging from 'Ranch' to 'Cape Cod' – with the result that individuality was lost, and a suburb in California was indistinguishable from one in Massachusetts.

Throughout the world the rise in the use of the motor car, along with the new demands of industry with automated techniques, needing more space, resulted in new town planning trends. People were moving out of the inner cities to the ever-growing, sprawling suburbs, and their old homes were being replaced by office blocks. This trend meant that vast areas of the world's major cities would be buzzing by day but empty by night and at the weekends. For example, in 1958 the City Planning Board of Boston, Massachusetts, commissioned a redevelopment plan for its city centre involving the demolition of 85% of the buildings and the elimination of all residential housing.

Similarly, the demands of the motor car meant that cities were beginning to be intersected by motorways, often cutting through historic areas without much concern about existing buildings. The importance of the car – ownership of which was beginning to be considered a necessity rather than a luxury in the 1950s and 1960s – was taken to extremes in the planning of new towns, such as Brazil's show-piece federal capital, Brasilia (designed by Lúcio Costa and Oscar Niemeyer from 1956 to the present) and Cumbernauld, near Glasgow, in Scotland. Both were planned from the beginning around the needs of the car. In Brasilia, for example, everyone is expected to drive not walk.

Overall, in the 1950s and 1960s, cities were becoming remarkably similar in appearance to some of Le Corbusier's totalitarian visions of high-rise planning as shown in such studies as the *Ville Radieuse* in 1930.

LEFT **'Tract' housing in the United States, 1950s**
One solution to the housing shortage which was in line with the American dream of a home for everyone.

RIGHT **Unité d'Habitation, Marseilles, France, Le Corbusier, 1946–52**
Le Corbusier's mass-housing scheme was to influence a generation of architects.

The idea of separating home life from work, zoning, and of moving housing out of the centre of cities, combined with the post-war population explosion, resulted in numerous schemes for new towns and 'projects'.

Britain's planners tackled the demand for housing, particularly in the south, by building from 1949 twelve new towns, eight of which were around London – Stevenage, Harlow, Welwyn Garden City, Hatfield, Hemel Hempstead, Bracknell, Crawley and Basildon.

Here the planners moved away from the strict rationalist rules of town planning, which aimed at order and rigid road patterns – along the lines of the American grid system – and went for a freer, more evolving, fluid design, with roads allowed to twist and turn in a more 'natural' fashion. The general feeling they were aiming for was evolution rather than uniformity – an idea taken a step further with the later development of Milton Keynes.

An important influence at this time was Modernism – which while previously a minority movement, now came to gain wide acceptance, particularly with governments, which saw its cheapness and seeming simplicity as a way around their limited resources and cash difficulties.

One of the most influential exponents of the pre-war Modern Movement, Le Corbusier was commissioned to design mass-housing projects. His Unité d'Habitation project at Marseilles in France (1946–52), a block of 337 flats which included a school, shops, laundry and communal areas, is the greatest practical realization of Le Corbusier's principles. The apartments, which were to house 1,600 inhabitants, were designed according to 23 styles, varying from a large family unit to a simple studio flat. The project, and particularly his use of raw concrete (Le Corbusier's favoured medium), aroused wide controversy, yet he was to influence a generation of architects – as can be seen from numerous housing developments around Europe such as the Grands Ensembles in France and such Italian schemes as the Forte di Quezzi residential quarter in Genoa (built 1960).

RIGHT **Stevenage, Hertfordshire, England**
Stevenage was the first new town to be designated under the British New Towns Act of 1946 and was planned to accommodate 80,000 residents.

BELOW **Brasilia, Brazil, Lucio Costa and Oscar Niemeyer, 1956–present**
Brazil's show-piece federal capital was designed for the car not the pedestrian.

Unfortunately, these followers did not always think through their plans to quite such a degree as Le Corbusier, with the result that the Modern Movement failed in the area which was most important to politicians and planners as well as architects – mass housing. Their predeliction for impersonal high-rise blocks discredited the movement in the eyes of the public and alienated a generation, turning architects into bogeymen for many.

Projects such as the Roehampton Estate in London and the Park Hill and Hyde Park estates in Sheffield, while winning initial praise and awards, did not find favour with the people who actually had to live in them. They felt isolated and under threat in their flats. The very size of such projects were felt to be intimidating – particularly for people used to little 'two up, two down' houses – and the walkways, or 'streets in the sky', while intended to provide meeting places which could engender community feelings, replacing the old doorsteps or garden walls as gossip areas, soon became desolate and windy no-go areas frequented by muggers and packs of dogs.

The precepts of the Modern Movement, which included such ideas as 'bigger is better', 'form follows function' and 'the expert knows best', did not endear the movement's exponents to the general public – who saw them as being removed from everyday life – and gradually the tide started to turn against the mass housing projects and the high-rise.

This feeling was summed up by journalist and critic Christopher Booker when he wrote: 'For the first time we had seen our future and it did not work. Our architectural and cultural self-confidence disintegrated with quite astounding speed.'

Events such as the partial collapse of the high-rise block Ronan Point in London in 1968 after a gas explosion (see Community Architecture) hardly settled the public's collective mind and gradually authorities, which had previously been so keen to erect high-rise blocks and huge projects, found themselves demolishing the very same buildings – often before they had even finished paying for their construction.

One notable example was the Pruitt-Igoe project in St Louis, Missouri. This was built between 1955 and 1958 to the design of Minoru Yamasaki (who also designed the World Trade Center in New York). Hailed as innovative at its conception, it was in 1972

LEFT **Milton Keynes, Buckinghamshire, England, 1967–present**

The later generation of New Towns, or in this case New Cities, shows planners' growing pre-occupation with the overall quality of life.

ABOVE **A failed experiment**
By the early 1970s, authorities throughout the world found themselves blowing up high-rise blocks they had previously thought were the cure to all their housing ills.

blown up due to the campaigns of its residents.

An alternative to the unpopular large developments was the renewal of existing housing stock – which made great sense for cities such as New York, whose West Side area was full of sub-standard 'Brownstone' houses. One of the advantages of re-development was that communities did not need to be split up or relocated and could be consulted about their needs or desires. This 'community' architecture allows people to have a direct influence on their environment.

One of the most successful of these schemes is the Byker Development in Newcastle-upon-Tyne in Britain (1968–81) by Ralph Erskine, Vernon Gracie and Roger Tillotson. Although a mass-housing scheme for 10,000 people, the architects sought the views of the future residents and even lived on-site, and their office, also on-site, became something of a social centre. The result is a low-rise scheme which has kept such familiar landmarks as pubs and churches, and which has attempted to mix shops and offices in with housing to provide a more normal and traditional way of living.

One of the keys to the success of the Byker Development seems to be the variety inherent in the project, and this avoidance on uniformity is also apparent in such successful schemes as Rue des Hautes-Formes in Paris, built between 1975–9 by Georgia Benamo and Christian de Port Zamparc. There are 209 apartments of which there are 18 types with 100 variations. All are in six buildings grouped around a street containing a central square.

On a larger scale, Milton Keynes in Britain (1967 to the present) also uses this technique of variety. This is a new city rather than a new town, conceived for a population of a quarter of a million. In a way it encapsulates many of the lessons learned in town planning and mass (though in a different sense of the word) housing. The planners have looked at the overall quality of life – and that means leisure and not just working life. They have come up with a plan that includes numerous parks and woods, rather than just bleak 'green spaces', and while the road system has been carefully thought out in traffic terms, the pedestrian has also been considered.

This consideration reflects an important international trend towards car-free areas – an early example was set by Bologna in Italy which, realizing in the late 1950s and early 1960s that its historic centre was being destroyed by cars, sought to preserve and restore the remainder and set up pedestrian precincts.

The past 30 years have seen extreme swings of attitudes and ideas as regards building for the masses. From the huge, brutal and dehumanizing high-rise blocks of the late 1950s and early 1960s, the fashion is now for smaller, lower and more varied schemes, with the specific needs of the family and of the community kept firmly in mind. It is now realized that it is not enough to provide people with warm, dry houses or flats. There must be something more, and that something must make people feel secure and part of a community. Isolation is out, quality of life is the new tenet.

CORPORATE STYLE

While Modernism had been the prerogative of a small number of intellectual enthusiasts in the 1920s and 1930s, its progressive designs became the acceptable face of modern architecture in the years following World War II. Corporate architecture, which by its very nature has to convey a sense of permanence and authority, welcomed the 'glass and steel' style with its potential for open-plan space and good lighting. Ironically, it proved to be capitalism that provided Modernism with one of its most successful formulae. Companies more often than not commissioned the style with an eye to prestige and individuality, but quite often ended up with largely anonymous buildings as the number of office buildings in the same style spiralled.

In the United States, the architectural firm of Skidmore, Owings and Merrill designed Lever House on New York's Park Avenue (1952). It used the device of a podium, as the Philadelphia Savings Fund Society had done before it, in order to visually link the verticality of the building to the horizontal lines of the ground.

LEFT **Lever House, New York, Skidmore, Owings & Merrill, 1952**
Sheathed in a largely transparent skin of tinted glass, this building set the trend in the design of large office blocks.

ABOVE **Pirelli Building, Milan, Italy, Gio Ponti, 1957**
Elegantly tapering at both sides and covered with metallic cladding, the Pirelli Building comprised 33 storeys around a core of lifts.

OPPOSITE **Seagram Building, New York, Ludwig Mies van der Rohe with Philip Johnson, 1954–8**
Mies van der Rohe's scheme for a glass office block in 1921 could not have been more prophetic; at the time it was structurally inconceivable, but within 35 years the idea had become a practicality.

ABOVE **Hancock Tower, Boston, Massachusetts, IM Pei and Associates/designer H Cobb, 1969–73**
Like Mies van der Rohe whom he admired, IM Pei was meticulous about using quality materials and the latest technology. This suited many of his corporate patrons who saw his highly refined architecture as a public relations exercise.

ABOVE RIGHT **City Hall, Boston, Massachusetts, Kallmann, McKinnell & Knowles, 1962–7**
The architects successfully managed to combine a sense of civic authority and openness by creating a monumental building, but one that was 'broken up' by means of perforations and a deep recess at ground level.

OPPOSITE **Yamanashi Press and Radio Centre, Kofu, Japan, Kenzo Tange, 1964–7**
The building has the appearance of a giant kit in which rooms or even entire floors can be added or subtracted at will. The cylindrical towers house the services of the building including stairs, lifts and air-conditioning.

Sheathed in reflective blue-green tinted glass, the effect of weightlessness and dematerialization is further enhanced by the absence of strong structural elements – horizontal and vertical elements are merely implied by thin banding.

The pioneer of 'steel and glass' architecture, Mies van der Rohe, settled in Chicago, the home of steel construction, but it was in New York that his major corporate work was built. The Seagram Building which Mies van der Rohe designed with Philip Johnson (1954–8) is of crucial significance in the development of

the office block; many hundreds of near copies were designed throughout the world in the following decades. The building was, in essence, the technical realization of Mies's glass tower of 35 years earlier, in that the basic structure was sheathed in glass with very little interruption of the silhouette. The building was set back from the road allowing a clear view from pedestrian level, and a horizontal slab indicated the entrance. Like all of Mies van der Rohe's buildings, quality craftsmanship was maintained throughout.

In Italy, Gio Ponti designed the elegant Pirelli Building in Milan (1957) which broke away from the Mies formula by incorporating bevelled sides, made possible by the double vertebrate system of construction. The 'glass and steel' block was used for a number of other purposes in addition to corporate offices during the 1950s, notably for the United Nations Building (1947–50) developed from an idea by Le Corbusier, the SAS Hotel in Copenhagen designed by Arne Jacobsen in 1958, the State buildings at Brasilia designed by Oscar Niemeyer (1957–60) and the New York State Theatre, Lincoln Centre, New York by Philip Johnson (1960).

During the 1960s the 'glass and steel' style was widely used for office blocks, but so too was a more architectonic sculptural style inspired by Le Corbusier's experiments with the plastic nature of concrete – particularly for organizations with the need to house

varied activities. In Japan, Kunio Mayekawa designed the Kyoto Town Hall (1958–60) in which the raw concrete had the surface appearance of wood and where the construction was a powerful feature of the design.

Kenzo Tange was commissioned to design headquarters for the Yamanashi Press and Radio Company in Kofu (1964–7). Huge concrete service towers delineate the building at the same time as providing the struts from which hang the various working spaces, including broadcasting studios and shops. The building has the appearance of being put together from a kit (it looks as if floors can be added or subtracted as necessary) and its technical wizardry has obviously affected the design – a characteristic that was to be explored in the 1970s and 1980s. G Kallmann, M McKinnell and E Knowles' design for the City Hall in Boston (1962–7), with its raw concrete monumentality, gave the city suitably 'corporate' headquarters.

The TWA terminal at Kennedy Airport, New York, designed by Eero Saarinen (1960) reveals a third, more expressive, sculptural approach. Massive curved planes sweep together, and flight is implied by the 'wings' of the roof. The purpose and shape of the rooms within are of little consequence to the form and façade which dominate all.

The corporate 'steel and glass' style reached its logical conclusion with the Hancock Tower in Boston designed by the firm of I M Pei and Associates (architect H Cobb) in 1969. Reflective glass provided a 'living' skin while the precision perfection of the steel mullion system provided the ultimate corporate slickness.

PUBLIC DEVELOPMENTS

The two decades following the war saw an unprecedented level of public building for education, the arts and other recreational facilities. As the tide of nationalism receded, and the task of rebuilding war-scarred cities started, civic pride manifested through new cathedrals of culture became an important focus of architectural activity.

There was a spate of new university building, notably in Britain, where the number of universities more than doubled as the government sought belatedly to catch up with the educational achievements of other Western countries.

BELOW **Barbican Centre, London – Chamberlin, Powell and Bon, 1959–81**
One of the largest post-war developments in London, the Barbican provides arts facilities, more than 2000 flats, and a conference centre.

Art galleries, concert halls, opera houses and theatres also sprang up in profusion throughout the prosperous United States and to a lesser extent, across Europe.

Modernism, a minority style before the war, and stifled by dictatorships, now became the architectural mainstream.

Le Corbusier's 1947 Unité d'Habitation project at Marseilles although a housing scheme, was to prove the source of a new aesthetic that became embedded in many 1950s and 1960s public developments.

The walls of the Unité were of *béton brut* – raw concrete that displayed the texture of the shuttering used in the forming process. Critics coined the word 'Brutalist' to denote Le Corbusier's assertion of his material and its expressive qualities.

Alison and Peter Smithson became the first of a line of British architects to adopt the term, and between 1949 and 1954 they built a Secondary School at Hunstanton in Norfolk that was

RIGHT **Royal Festival Hall, London, London County Council, 1951**
The first and most outstanding building in the South Bank complex, the Royal Festival Hall makes full use of the River Thames with its extensive glass facade and numerous balconies.

ROYAL FESTIVAL HALL

OPPOSITE **Engineering Faculty, Leicester University, James Stirling, 1959–63**
Stirling's choice of a tower to house laboratories and workshops was an unconventional one, but the extensive industrial glazing was a practical way to provide maximum lighting.

loosely based on a Mies van der Rohe design, but which exposed steelwork, brickwork, floor beams as well as service fittings such as plumbing.

Brutalism became largely synonymous with the use of massive slabs of concrete through such developments as London's South Bank arts complex and the shopping centre at Cumbernauld – a new town built near Glasgow, once seen as a brave new world and now derelict.

Although variously admired for their qualities of sculpture and composition, each has also been severely criticized for the alienation caused by creating 'ghettos' which were isolated rather than connected by pedestrian walkways.

James Stirling, initially with his partner James Gowan, became another disciple of Brutalism, using glass instead of concrete as the main expressive material of his Engineering Faculty tower at Leicester University (1959–64) and his History Faculty Library in Cambridge (1964–9). One unfortunate miscalculation has been to create a 'greenhouse' effect in areas of both buildings, where sweltering conditions make it difficult for students to work.

One of the first important buildings to be erected in Europe after the war was London's Royal Festival Hall, which was completed in time for the Festival of Britain in 1951. Behind its exten-

ABOVE **Guggenheim Museum, New York, Frank Lloyd Wright, 1943–59**
More like a multi-storey car-park than a museum from its outward appearance, the Guggenheim's characteristic form has become a visual icon in its own right.

sive glass front looking onto the Thames, the building provided substantial areas of open space for the public, while the main auditorium was designed with a number of innovative acoustic features such as an absorbent membrane fitted under each seat, wooden panelling around the orchestra and a leather-padded wall surface at the rear.

Since in most European countries the immediate need was to concentrate on clearing bomb-sites and building cheap housing, it is no surprise that much of the interesting public architecture in the immediate post-war years emerged on the other side of the Atlantic. One of the first important post-war projects to be undertaken in the United States was Frank Lloyd Wright's Guggenheim Museum in New York. From first designs in 1943, the Guggenheim was started in 1945 but only completed 14 years later, after a decade of impasse.

The finished building, while not entirely true to the original plans, was revolutionary as an art gallery. Instead of arranging the walls for pictures around a conventional rectangular interior, Wright devised a completely original space, an ascending spiral ramp that expanded as it climbed upwards.

It was the outcome of a preoccupation with ramps that Wright had nurtured for many years, and which had been manifested in previous designs ranging from a giant car park to a department store. The central space of the Guggenheim was also reminiscent of Wright's Larkin Building in Buffalo, NY, of 1905.

Between 1947 and 1948, the Finnish architect Alvar Aalto made his one important contribution to American post-war architecture with the Baker House residence hall at the Massachusetts Institute of Technology. In Aalto's pre-war work in Finland, he had developed an original style featuring curved walls, single pitched roofs and traditional materials like brick and timber.

LEFT **TWA Terminal, Kennedy Airport, New York, Eero Saarinen, 1956–62**
The functionalism of early Modernism and the International Style has been replaced by dramatic impact.

OPPOSITE **Carpenter Center for the Visual Arts, Harvard, Le Corbusier, 1960**
Le Corbusier's individualistic style never attracted the popularity in America that it had in Europe.

Baker House was marked out from more orthodox halls of residence by the use of long diagonal stairways, which, together with the space above, projected from the main wall of the building. It also had an undulating façade which alluded to the nearby river.

One of the architects influenced by Aalto was Louis Kahn, who introduced a 'New Monumentalism' to the United States with buildings like the Yale University Art Gallery of 1951–3 and the Richards Medical Research Building at Philadelphia of 1960. Kahn was equally influenced by classical buildings and by formal grid systems of design, which led him to divide units of space into those which were 'servers' and those which were 'served'.

The approach of another prominent architect of this time, Eero Saarinen, was much more concerned with the plastic qualities of concrete, and owed a certain amount to German pre-war Expressionism. Saarinen designed buildings with large, dramatically curved roof spans such as the Yale Hockey Rink of 1958, or the TWA Terminal at Kennedy Airport, which Saarinen designed the following year.

A third Scandinavian architect, Jørn Utzon, made his mark alongside Aalto and Saarinen around this time, albeit on the other side of the world. Utzon won the competition in 1956 to design an opera house for the Australian city of Sydney.

The resulting building was finished in 1973 after Utzon had resigned in acrimonious circumstances, and its design had been rescued from the impossible by the structural genius of engineer Ove Arup. Despite that crisis, it is an outstanding example of how civic pride can be engendered in a single piece of architecture. Constructed on a promontory extending into Sydney harbour, the opera house has a roof consisting of giant sail-like concrete structures reminiscent of Saarinen's TWA Terminal, used purely for effect and not for functional reasons.

A somewhat different and more 'Brutalist' use of concrete showed itself in the United States, first, with Le Corbusier's Carpenter Visual Arts Center at Harvard, built in 1960, then with Paul Rudolph's Art and Architecture Building at Yale begun the following year.

The Carpenter, Le Corbusier's only building to be completed in the United States, employed many of his stock motifs, including a concrete grid framework and *brise soleils* (shade-making elements) and sat a little awkwardly alongside its predominantly red-brick neighbours at Harvard.

Rudolph's building at Yale, on the other hand, employed massive columns of textured, reinforced concrete in a labyrinthine composition of towers and terraces that anticipated some Brutalist developments in Britain.

America's wealth may have made possible some of the world's most significant new architecture after the war, but a number of innovative buildings were appearing in Europe too. Aalto, one of the most prolific architects of the period, completed a number of municipal developments in his native Finland, using materials ranging from white marble to wood, which were distinguished by their use of natural lighting, and by their carefully planned layout.

In Italy, Pier Luigi Nervi further developed the remarkable concrete rib structures he had experimented with before the war, in a completely enclosed circular stadium for the 1960 Olympics in Rome. Nervi considered himself an engineer, and his expertise in the use of concrete was called upon in a series of commissions, including the UNESCO headquarters in Paris.

From the point of view of internal organization, Hans Scharoun's Philharmonic Hall in Berlin, completed in 1963, is one of the most innovative cultural buildings of the post-war years. Although unremarkable from outside, the auditorium consists of seats arranged in sloping tiers, likened by Scharoun to flower beds, which completely surround the orchestra and its conductor.

In Britain during the 1960s, the most important development was the construction of the newly erected, 'red-brick' universities. One group, known as the Shakespearean Seven and consisting of Sussex, East Anglia, York, Lancaster, Essex, Warwick and Kent, were all built in the four years between 1961 and 1965.

They were characterized by being situated in parkland at some distance outside the nearest urban area, a feature that was later to prove controversial when it was realized that this effectively isolated the students from the life of the town.

In architectural terms, the two most outstanding are Sussex, designed by Sir Basil Spence on a theme of red brick interspersed

OPPOSITE ABOVE **Falmer House, University of Sussex, Sir Basil Spence, 1962**
The main building in the university complex, it is derivative of a fortified castle complete with central courtyard and surrounding moat.

OPPOSITE BELOW **Yale Art Gallery, Connecticut, Louis Kahn, 1951–53**
One of the buildings which helped Kahn to re-establish Monumentalism as a force in America after the war.

with concrete horizontals and segmental arches, and Dennis Lasdun and Partners' University of East Anglia, best known for its ziggurat-style halls of residence.

Although unlike any that had preceded them, the new British universities often retained clues to their origins in medieval colleges with features such as cloistered courtyards, and they were generally dignified, even Monumental, in character.

Finally, Modernism spread further afield for the first time in the post-war period. In Japan an indigenous tradition arose and gained international recognition. Kunio Maekewa, one of a number of Japanese architects who had worked in the office of Le Corbusier, built Festival Halls at Tokyo and Kyoto in 1960 and 1961, using massive concrete and displaying neo-Classical influences.

Kenzo Tange is best-known for the two stadia he built for the Tokyo Olympics in 1964 making exciting use of elliptical concrete roof-forms, suspended with the help of steel.

ABOVE **Supreme Court, Chandigarh, Punjab, Le Corbusier, 1951–56**
A building designed for the Indian climate, with *brise-soleils* and a canopy-like roof to give protection against both sun and monsoon.

Modernism came to the Indian sub-continent in the shape of Le Corbusier's epic commission to build a new capital for the Punjab at Chandigarh as well as some housing at Ahmedabad. Le Corbusier's most striking building at Chandigarh is the Law Courts, a rich composition of grilles and columns enclosed in a rectangular box, and reflected in front in two well-proportioned lakes divided by a causeway. Chandigarh has been judged by some to have achieved Monumentality outside of a Western tradition.

The other epic commission of the 1950s was for Brasilia, the new capital of Brazil. Oscar Niemeyer and Lucio Costa's city, still not entirely completed, combined its own version of Monumentality with a gracefulness that has seldom been bettered.

1970
1990

INTRODUCTION 1970–1990

While the 1970s saw architecture languishing in the doldrums, by the 1980s it had been rehabilitated, in fact by the middle of the decade it had gone one step further and from being acceptable had become downright fashionable.

Smart clothes and 'designer' goods shops from New York to Paris and London to Tokyo, proudly displayed copies of the more stylish architectural magazines beside their Comme des Garçons and Alessi wares, and such celebrated buildings as Richard Rogers' Paris Pompidou Centre featured on record covers. Shops also sprang up to deal with the new vogue for architect-designed consumer goods and some architects found that they were better known for their kettle design than for their latest building.

People began to drop the names of architectural movements and their exponents at supper parties. New York's Museum of Modern Art and London's Royal Academy ran major architectural exhibitions and even the heir to the throne of England got in on the act – causing controversy with his remarks about monstrous carbuncles, and attracting the wrath of the profession and admiration of his people for what many felt to be his rather reactionary taste. Having tapped a popular vein the public was not satisfied with newspaper coverage for his 'proclamations' and he even appeared on television and wrote a book, *The Vision of Britain*, about his ideas.

In many ways the International Style and Modern Movements (Prince Charles's bugbear), had brought this torrent of criticism down upon themselves with their puritanical, Bauhaus-influenced approach to architecture, in which function was all-important.

The buildings that resulted from this philosophy were intended to change people for the better, but only succeeded in alienating their inhabitants and discrediting the movements and modern architecture in general. Indeed, instead of improving the lot of the working class the Modern Movement's low-cost housing actually worsened it until the social problems resulting grew too great to be ignored and conformity began to be replaced by individualism.

After the economic recession of the 1970s, when many large building projects suffered, some indeed were abandoned, the 1980s saw a resurgence. In France the President Francois Mitterrand instigated a series of spectacular projects which would leave a physical reminder of his administration for posterity. In Britain, London's Docklands became the largest building site in Europe and in the United States various imaginative schemes were launched to regenerate inner city areas and city centres.

Various new patrons also appeared on the scene anxious to encourage the new talent and vibrancy. While private or individual patronage had all but disappeared (apart from a few brave entrepreneurs such as Peter Palumbo in Britain), companies such as Sainsbury's in Britain and Doug Tompkins' Esprit in the United States became keen to be associated with the new architecture. Esprit used, among others, Shiro Kuromata, Joe D'urso, Ettore Sottsass and Norman Foster, and Sainsbury's caused some controversy with the choice of architects such as Nicholas Grimshaw whose 'high tech' work many felt was not in keeping with food retailing. But as Richard Rogers said: 'Modern architecture cannot be separated from modern life – it is part of life.' A fact which many people may have felt was a pity as they struggled to get to grips with the plethora of architectural movements and changing styles and theories.

As the 1980s come to a close with architecture making news headlines, it will be interesting to see what developments occur as we approach the end of the century. Will all this attention and enthusiasm lead to a new approach to architecture or will stagnation reign and such extremes as Minimalism or Traditionalism take over?

CHARLES: OUR RUINED CITY...

ABOVE **Canary Wharf, London, in 1988**
London's Docklands – Europe's largest building site.

OPPOSITE **Headline news, 1988**
The heir to the throne of England has his say.

ABOVE RIGHT **John Hancock Tower, Boston, Massachusetts, IM Pei, 1969–73**
Reflecting glass enforces a feeling of separation from the surrounding world and emphasizes the soaring simplicity of this building.

RIGHT **Saint Edward's College, London, Aloysius Peel, 1980**
Traditional materials, such as slate and brick, are once again finding favour with architects willing to learn from vernacular architecture, adapting old techniques to modern styles.

HIGH TECH

High Tech architecture has been described as the second machine aesthetic by architectural critic Charles Jencks. And while many high tech buildings owe a great deal more to the futurist visions of the 1960s 'pop' architecture group Archigram, which put forward plans for 'walking' and 'plug-in' cities, the movement was foreshadowed by almost 100 years by the Eiffel Tower in Paris. For the ideas behind the Eiffel Tower (which caused a storm of protest in its day) and a high tech building such as the Pompidou Centre (another Parisian building to cause a storm), are patently similar. In both structures the skeleton of the building is on display, both are celebrations of technology.

That does not mean to say that the technology used is necessarily more advanced than that used in any other recent architectural movement, just that it is put on display and used to give the building a framework and character. In nearly all High Tech architecture this framework is deliberately designed to be flexible, so that the buildings can be either added to or reduced. For example, Norman Foster's Renault Building in Swindon (1982) consists of an aluminium-skinned series of canopies made up of yellow steel

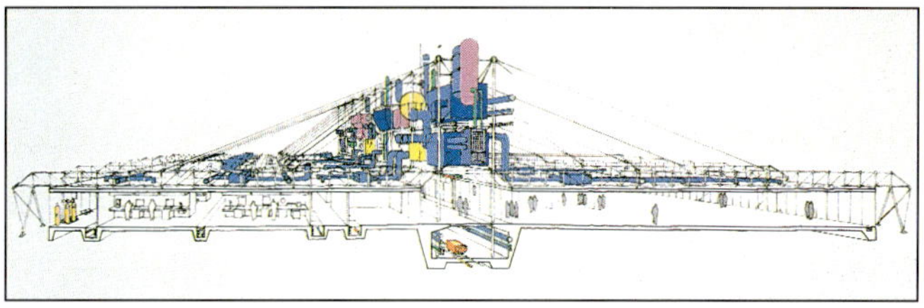

OPPOSITE ABOVE **Pompidou Centre, Paris, Richard Rogers & Renzo Piano, 1971–7**
Described by its architects as 'a giant Meccano set', the Pompidou Centre caused a storm of controversy, much as that engendered by the bold skeletal structure of the Eiffel Tower (Gustave Eiffel, 1889) – a clear precursor of the High Tech movement (OPPOSITE BELOW).

ABOVE LEFT **Inmos Microprocessor Factory, Gwent, Wales, Richard Rogers, 1982**
The High Tech style was particularly appropriate for such an advanced technological industry. The sunken duct under the central spine shown in the sketch (LEFT) was later abandoned.

masts with cables extending out to struts. The whole structure can be dismantled or added to, to provide more storage, office or exhibition space.

In the case of Richard Rogers' and Renzo Piano's Pompidou Centre (1971–1977) the internal spaces can be altered – in their own words they wanted: 'A giant Meccano set rather than a traditional, static, transparent or solid doll's house.'

The use of colour is also important in High Tech, yet although the colours used tend to be primary, as in Post-Modernism they are used for practical as opposed to just ornamental purposes. Rogers and Foster use colour to code the service pipes and ducts which are on the outside of their buildings. The colour coding chosen for the Pompidou Centre was red, white and blue – making a French tricolour.

Placing the services on the external shell makes maintenance easier and High Tech buildings are in the main designed to be cheap, easy and quick to construct, as one of the earliest UK examples, Foster's advance head office for IBM in Hampshire (1971), shows. This practicality is also obvious in such buildings as the Inmos Factory in Gwent by Richard Rogers (1982). The High Tech style was particularly appropriate for such an advanced technology industry – computer chip manufacture. Rogers' tent-like structure, with its central raised spine and masts from which come cables supporting steel trusses, is echoed in Michael Hopkins' 1984 Schlumberger Research Institute in Cambridge, which in the words of British architect Eva Jiřićna is 'like a big top'.

The Hongkong & Shanghai Bank in Hong Kong (1979–86) by Norman Foster has been called the ultimate High Tech building. On a prime water-front site, it is made up of three slabs, all at different heights, so that although it looks like a solid rectangle from the front, from the side it looks rather like a fairy-tale castle with thin towers like pinnacles soaring to the sky. The bank has an atrium at its core and throughout the inside of the building the X-shaped struts or trusses provide a strong motif as well as a reminder of its construction.

One of the most recently opened High Tech buildings is by Richard Rogers – who was once in partnership with Foster. It is the Lloyd's Building in London (1978–86). Although in the heart of the City, it does not attempt to blend in with any of the surrounding buildings but instead stands out with its 'inside out' construction. Rogers has put all the services into towers which surround, but are separated from, the main building with its central atrium. This atrium, which goes the full height of the building, provides a central core around which the offices are grouped – from the outside it looks like a Victorian conservatory – and provides an amusing and effective contrast to the rest of

LEFT **Lloyd's Building, London, Richard Rogers, 1978–86**
Service towers surround the main part of the building, the core of which consists of an atrium with offices grouped around it.

RIGHT & FAR RIGHT **Hongkong & Shanghai Bank, Hong Kong, Norman Foster, 1979–86**
The interior shows the cross struts which are the basis of its construction. The building is made up of three rectangular slabs, or towers, of varying heights.

RIGHT **Sainsbury Centre, University of East Anglia, England, Norman Foster, 1978**
Foster has used a double skin to hide the working parts of the building as well as to provide insulation inside a sleek exterior.

the façade. Although a concrete construction, the façade is surfaced with steel and glass which, with all the services on the outside, creates a glittering surface by day and a dramatic silhouette by night.

Norman Foster's earlier Sainsbury Centre For The Visual Arts at the University of East Anglia, UK (1978) also has a glass and metal exterior, yet this early High Tech building has avoided putting all its working parts on display by creating a double-skin to contain all the pipes as well as to provide insulation, the result is very sleek and delicate, while still remaining distinctly High Tech.

The impression of technological supremacy so evident in buildings such as Lloyds and the Hongkong and Shanghai Bank is important for the image of power and, above all, wealth that these institutions wish to project. Similarly High Tech architecture can suggest a feeling of advancement and efficiency, as in Schlumberger or Inmos, or playfulness and creativity – Pompidou and Sainsbury – making it a supremely flexible style, both physically and in the different images it can be adapted to.

POST-MODERNISM – THE NEW INTERNATIONAL STYLE

Post-Modernism arose out of a general worldwide loss of confidence in the International Modern Movement and a realization of its inadequacies. People were becoming bored and alienated by the severe cubic shapes and abstract geometry of Modernism. It was too uniform and lacked any sort of historical reference which could provide a feeling of continuity – an idea of place, time and, above all, identity. After this severity the public was ready for more variety, it wanted signs of individuality and even frivolity.

OPPOSITE ABOVE **Mother's House, Philadelphia, Robert Venturi, 1962–4**
One of the first buildings to make the bold move away from the cubes and right angles of most Modernist architecture.

OPPOSITE BELOW **Piazza d'Italia, New Orleans, Louisiana, Charles Moore, 1975–80**
A light-hearted development, dedicated to the local Italian community.

The term Post-Modernism was coined in the 1970s, possibly first by the architectural critic Charles Jencks in his 1977 book *The Language of Post-Modern Architecture*. He defined Post-Modernism as a 'Populist-Pluralist art of immediate communicability'. The 1980 exhibition 'The Presence of the Past' – as part of the Venice Biennale encapsulated the feelings and style of the movement in the main exhibit, the *'Strada Nuovissima'*. This was a street consisting of 20 façades which had been designed by, among others, Robert Venturi, Charles Moore, Ricardo Bofill, Hans Hollein and Leon Krier. This 'street' contained some of the design characteristics now commonly associated with Post-Modernism, in particular Classical orders used in an exaggerated, playful way.

ABOVE **AT&T headquarters, New York, Philip Johnson, 1978–84**
This was the building which brought Post-Modernism to the attention of the world. Its broken pediment has now been so widely copied that it has become a cliché.

LEFT **Staatsgalerie extension, Stuttgart, James Stirling and Michael Wilford, 1977–84**
Classical elements and primary colours combine to provide a gallery as exciting as the art it exhibits.

OPPOSITE **Portland Public Services Building, Oregon, Michael Graves, 1979–82**
This building draws upon influences and styles as varied as Classical, Egyptian and Art Deco.

This playfulness is important to the movement. Post-Modernism has been described as theatrical and kitschy, it is also said to be trying to create instant or neo-History. Indeed its practitioners do employ columns, pediments and rustication as a sort of 'coding'. The use of gaudy colours – especially primary ones – is all part of the lack of seriousness. For example in some buildings the Classical orders are there, but are made from such materials as neon or bright metal. On the AT&T headquarters in New York (1978–84) by Philip Johnson – considered by many to be the high priest of Post-Modernism – the broken pediment in the Chippendale style on top of the skyscraper seems to be part of a private joke – a joke which has been so widely copied that it has become a cliché.

Perhaps the extreme example of Post-Modernist architecture is the Piazza d'Italia in New Orleans, Louisiana. Designed by the arch-exponent of the style, Charles Moore, between 1975 and 1980 for the local Italian community, it has as its focal point a fountain in the shape of Italy, with water running down along the rivers Po, Tiber and Arno. Moore has used each of the five Italian orders and, in the manner of medieval craftsman has incorporated his face on one wall of the fountain, spouting water from the mouth. The materials he has used include marble, stainless steel, neon and brick, and the overall effect is that of a brightly lit and painted ruined temple dedicated to some god of mischief or chaos.

Michael Graves's Portland Public Service Building at Portland, Oregon (1979–82) draws not just upon the Classical tradition but also on Egyptian and Art Deco styles. It expresses the spirit of Pluralism in materials and themes (which Jencks talks about), so important in American Post-Modernism. Like Moore's Piazza d'Italia, it mixes different materials, styles and colours. Originally Graves wanted to drape the building with huge fibre-glass garlands, but public outcry caused him to abandon the idea.

In Europe, the Post-Modern spirit is encapsulated in Taller (meaning 'studio') de Arquitectura by Ricardo Bofill. Les Espaces d'Abraxus (1978–84) housing development in the new town of Marne-la-Vallée, 10 miles outside Paris. Made up of three blocks – Theatre, Palace and Triumphal Arch – the design draws upon Classicism with columns and pilasters, yet uses the latest engineering techniques and materials, such as pre-cast concrete, to create a massive stage set, with the development's residents as the cast.

James Stirling resists being categorized, and particularly hates the Post-Modernist tag, even if his architecture is defined as Post-Modern-*Classical* rather than just Post-Modern. Yet in his intricate extension to the Staatsgalerie at Stuttgart, designed with Michael Wilford (1977–84), and displaying influences that range from De Stijl through Le Corbusier to Alvar Aalto, his familiar use of striped rustication – travertine and sandstone – together with painted metal awnings in red, blue and yellow, and the central 'domeless dome' (an outdoor sculpture gallery), an 18th-century portico and an Egyptian cornice, place it as unmistakeably Post-Modern.

NEO-CLASSICAL AND TRADITIONAL

It is fascinating to reconstruct the past, especially when this can be done in bricks and mortar. In Britain, the maverick architect Clough Williams Ellis did just this with Portmeirion (1933–1972), his pastiche of a Mediterranean port, modelled on Portofino in Italy and built in the unlikely setting of the North Wales coast.

More recently in the United States, a group of architects including Neuerburg, Langdon and Wilson, built the John Paul Getty Museum in Malibu, California (1970–1975), a reconstruction of a Roman villa uncovered at Herculaneum.

Post-Modernism employs many Classical elements – columns, pediments and arches for example – but its frivolity and somewhat toy-town appearance puts it on a much more transitory plane than traditional architecture, whether that be vernacular or Classical.

Post-Modernist architecture has an element of fashion about it which makes it liable to have a built-in time limit of acceptability. Its very difference could cause its attractions to pall, and people may grow tired of it. In a reaction against this the Traditional and neo-Classical movements have evolved which adopt a more serious, long-term approach to architecture.

Early signs of this return to tradition are apparent in the work of architects such as Robert Venturi, yet the style has now developed to such an extent that, like Portmeirion and the Getty Museum, what is being built could be described as reproduction architecture – an old shell on a modern interior.

The extension to the Old Bailey law courts in London by McMorran and Whitby (1972) won approval for its Classical look, yet still remained a recognizably modern building, but the Landesbibliothek in Karlsruhe, West Germany, by Oswald Mathias Ungers (1979–1985) could easily be mistaken for an old building with its colonnaded facade and pitched roof.

The gradual abandonment of Modern Movement ideals in favour of a more traditional look may be directly connected with the architectural conservation movement, which received a boost in Europe with a 1975 exhibition in London entitled 'The destruction of the country house'. This showed that in Britain alone no fewer than 1,000 historic houses had been wholly or partly destroyed since 1908.

People were reminded of how industry and economic development had affected old buildings throughout the world. The determination to protect what remained was strengthened, and the popular success of architects such as Raymond Erith, John Simpson, Leon Krier, Alan Greenberg and perhaps the one

synonymous with the movement, Quinlan Terry, was assured.

Quinlan Terry claims that Modernism was: 'The avoidance of every method that has hitherto worked.' By contrast he feels the Classical orders are divinely inspired. He cites Erith as his mentor and indeed worked with him on buildings such as a house in Hertfordshire, Kings Waldenburg, in 1970. He later went on to design buildings such as Dufours Place in London (1984) – inspired by 18th-century models – the Howard Building at Downing College in Cambridge, England (1987) and his biggest project to date, a development in Richmond, London (opened 1989).

The Richmond development, on the banks of the Thames, is on the inside a modern office block with all the technology that requires, yet its exterior looks as though it was created a couple of hundred years ago and it has been standing there untouched. It is instant history with all modern conveniences, although its more avid supporters should beware because, in the words of Richard Rogers, 'A society more interested in the past than the future is a dying society.'

OPPOSITE & RIGHT **Two faces of Quinlan Terry**
The Richmond Development, London, 1989 – instant history with all the modern conveniences, and (right) Thenford, Northamptonshire, a new, old-style country house.

BELOW **Portmeirion, North Wales, Clough Williams Ellis, 1933–72**
One man's dream of a Mediterranean port became reality on the Welsh coastline.

DECONSTRUCTIVISM

In 1988 the Museum of Modern Art in New York put on an exhibition entitled 'Deconstructivist Architecture'. Under the aegis of veteran American architect, Philip Johnson, the show featured six architects and one practice, and for many it was the first they had heard of 'Deconstructivist' or 'Deconstruction' architecture – there is some argument as to the correct term.

The architects involved were Bernard Tschumi, Frank Gehry and Peter Eisenman, all of whom were based in the United States; Daniel Libeskind, based in Italy; Rem Koolhaas, in Holland; Zaha Hadid, in Britain; and the Austrian Coop Himmelblau practice.

The exhibition stressed that Deconstructivist architecture was not a new style, nor was it a creed, or even a movement. Instead it stated that this architecture harked back to the Russian Constructivists of the 1920s and 1930s. But the uniting theme in all the pieces could be summed up in the quote displayed at the entrance to the exhibition: 'Pure form has indeed been contaminated, transforming architecture into an agent of instability, disharmony and conflict.' As Mark Wigley, the Associate Curator explained, architecture is a conservative discipline producing pure form, while in Deconstructivism this dream of pure form is disturbed and becomes a nightmare.

In practise the architecture that results from this nightmare consists of a bewildering collection of haphazardly-placed planes and twisted lines which all combine to create an impression that the structure is about to collapse. Needless to say, many of the buildings never make the transition from the drawing-board to the building site.

While as early as 1961 Herbe Greene was experimenting with such eccentric buildings as his own house, at Norman, Oklahoma it was not until 1978 that Frank Gehry took this shanty-town style to suburbia with his addition to an ordinary Santa Monica house. He has used such unlikely materials as chain-link fencing, corrugated steel, glass and asphalt, to create an extension which has so many different angles that it is very disorientating, and has been described by a neighbour as 'a dirty thing to do in someone else's front yard'.

But while Gehry's house didn't prove popular locally, the Notch

Project in Sacramento, California, produced a year earlier in 1977 by James Wines and SITE, took the jokey side of Deconstructivism to create 'De-Architecture', with the Best building – a project which does seem to be going down well. This store looks at first sight like a bare brick box, that is until opening time when one corner of the building, a 45-ton wedge, separates from the rest and moves 40 ft (12 m) to reveal the entrance. The shoppers are said to love it.

Another building to make it from the second to the third dimension is Peter Eisenman's House VI, which has a disturbing gap, or invisible column, which runs all the way up through the house, even separating the beds in the master-bedroom. He has also placed an inverted staircase above the real one, creating a dizzying effect. In his House X, Eisenman has gone one stage further, using glass floors and avoiding giving the house any obvious centre.

The general public's first exposure to Deconstructivist architecture on any scale is Eisenman's joint scheme with Bernard Tschumi for the Parc de la Villette, part of President Mitterrand's 'Grands Projets' for Paris. Together they have created a series of strange-looking red buildings, full of flying beams and odd angles called, appropriately, *folies* (a pun on the English follies and the French word meaning mad). It remains to be seen whether this park will help the movement win public recognition.

RIGHT & BELOW RIGHT **Santa Monica, California, Frank Gehry, 1978**
Shanty-town style hits suburbia with a disorientating mix of angles and materials.

OPPOSITE **House VI, USA, Peter Eisenman**
An invisible column runs up the middle of the house drawing the eye upwards, yet disturbing the intellect.

EPIC COMMISSIONS

It must be the ultimate ambition of every architect to be given an epic commission – the chance to design something not necessarily large, but of great importance on a key site which will attract immense public attention.

Some practices get more than their fair share of opportunities, for example the practice of Philip Johnson and John Burgee in the United States has proved very popular with commercial and financial clients and has produced major projects such as Pennzoil Place in Houston, Texas (1974–1975) – a pair of diagonally-topped wedge shaped buildings; the Post Oak Central Building, also in Houston (1974–1976); Thanksgiving Square in Dallas, Texas (1977), a slick, black, glass-fronted building with the blank, anonymous façade so appropriate for big business; and, of course, the AT&T building in New York (1978–1982), which with its use of the Chippendale tallboy split pediment has the novel effect of associating something old with one of the most technological of American corporations.

It is the large multi-national companies which tend to be the main patrons nowadays. After all there are not many super-rich individuals who can afford to commission very large projects – with the exception of New York's Donald Trump of course, whose Trump Tower (by Der Scutt, 1979) is a monument to himself – and those able to put their money and trust in architects have often found their way blocked. Peter Palumbo in Britain, for example, has been trying to develop his Mansion House Square site, for decades. His original project, for a Mies van der Rohe skyscraper, met with stiff opposition and was rejected despite appeals, as was his second proposal – for a development by James Stirling. Both victims of the public's dislike of and distrust for the International Style and the Modern Movement in general.

Private development companies will obviously commission architects – London's Docklands has seen a rash of large private projects, in the main unhampered by building or planning controls. But even there the restraining hand of government bodies will step in if the architectural project looks like getting totally out of hand. For example, the developers of the £2-billion Canary Wharf project have, rightly, had to go through numerous hoops before being granted approval for the Anglo-American joint-design team from Yorke, Rosenberg and Mardell with Skidmore, Owings and Merrill.

The state still commissions schemes other than housing and it is the commissions for cultural centres, such as art galleries, opera houses or theatres, which receive most public scrutiny. The architects for many of these projects are chosen on the basis of the work they submit to a competition panel. Richard Rogers'

OPPOSITE Pennzoil Place, Houston, Texas, Philip Johnson and John Burgee, 1974–5
Anonymous, wedge shapes proclaim corporate power.

RIGHT Trump Tower, New York, Der Scutt, 1979
A monument to one man and his money.

BELOW Pompidou Centre, Paris, Renzo Piano and Richard Rogers, 1971–7
A people's palace whose popular success confounded its critics.

and Rienzo Piano's winning design for the Beaubourg (better known as the Pompidou Centre), in Paris was one of 700 completed entries for a world-wide competition to create 'a people's palace'. What was eventually built proved very controversial but popular – and controversy seems to dog cultural commissions. The extension to the National Gallery in London caused rows which went on for years until the job was finally awarded to Robert Venturi – although even that caused a storm as he was an American. James Stirling's extension to London's Tate Gallery, the Clore Gallery built to house the Turner Collection (1987), also provoked many strongly-worded articles in the press as well as television debates.

Stirling had already proved himself, however, with his extension to the Stuttgart Staatsgalerie (1977–84) which has proved as much a draw to visitors as the exhibition staged within (see Post-Modernism).

The extension to the Louvre in Paris (1988), like the Stuttgart Staatsgalerie, makes no attempt to blend with the buildings surrounding it. In fact it is debatable whether Ieoh Ming Pei's transparent glass pyramid could strictly be called an extension as it is placed in the middle of the 17th century Jardin du Carousel rather than being directly attached to the Louvre. The pyramid, 70 ft (21 m) high and surrounded by three much smaller satellite pyramids, is in fact the entrance to an underground complex, built at a cost of £100 million. This complex provides routes to each of the Louvre's wings, and the pyramids (the smaller of which are skylights for these underground corridors) have the added attraction that they look like pieces of sculpture through which one can see the old buildings.

Besides building monuments to art, I M Pei has also constructed cathedrals to commerce, one of the best-known of which is the Hancock Tower in Boston, Massachusetts (1967–1975), which uses the idea of a whole structure being made up of individual parts – in this case twin towers. It is an idea or method that has been well used in large buildings as different as Roche and Dinkeloo's One UN Plaza, New York (1969–76), Richard Rogers' Lloyd's Building in London (1978–86) and Norman Foster's Hongkong & Shanghai Bank in Hong Kong (1979–86) (see High Tech for fuller descriptions).

All these buildings act as reflections of the power and prestige of the companies they house. Like a medieval castle they warn the onlooker of the might of their occupants and their invincibility, and while art galleries and other cultural centres are designed to be approachable and to stimulate, the image commercial institutions seek to convey in the buildings they commission is permanence and impersonality.

It is interesting to compare the variety of styles used for museums and galleries with the relative uniformity of commercial architecture. The images cultural commissions project, are much more individual and architecture is used as a means of communication, in contrast to the blank silence of much commercial architecture.

LEFT **One UN Plaza, New York, Roche, Dinkeloo and Associates, 1967–76**
Twin towers are used to break up the dull uniformity of a single block.

RIGHT **Clore Gallery, London, James Stirling, 1987**
An extension to the Tate built to house the Turner collection, it provoked many strongly worded articles.

BELOW **Louvre extension, Paris, IM Pei, 1988**
A striking contrast between old and new yet each complements the other.

REDEVELOPMENT AND RENOVATION

Despite occasional well-publicized 'mistakes' and the dubious fast work of developers (such as the rather rushed demolition of the Art Deco Firestone factory in London one Bank Holiday weekend in 1980, just before it was due to be listed), there had tended to be a swing away from the mass demolition of buildings so popular in the 1950s and 1960s. Instead developers are taking a more thoughtful approach – influenced no doubt by strong public feeling and the better organized approach of the conservationists world-wide.

The conservation movement has been around for many decades but until some of the excesses of the 1960s it had tended to be dismissed as consisting of cranks. It was only when various schemes of the Modern Movement failed so dramatically in the public's eyes, particularly the large housing developments, and when some very familiar, if not necessarily popular, landmarks were pulled down to make way for new projects (for example London's Euston Arch, designed by Philip Hardwick in the 19th century), that people began to lose trust in the judgement of planners and architects. They came to realize that fiscal

ABOVE & OPPOSITE **Guinness Hop Store, Dublin, Ireland**
The successful conversion into museum and gallery showed how easily large, old warehouses work as exhibition spaces.

LEFT **Bristol Docks, Britain**
Being, unusually, in the centre of the city, the docks' redevelopment – including shops, workshops, radio station and gallery – proved an immediate draw.

considerations – all-important to developers – did not necessarily make for improved environments.

So planners and developers began to look at how they could create new offices, shops, leisure centres and housing without totally destroying the look and feel of an area. The answer was re-using old buildings for different purposes. This was particularly sensible in certain areas, such as in London's Docklands, where circumstances – the decline of the shipping industry – had rendered the buildings redundant. Similarly the movement of industry outside capital cities left large premises empty which could quite easily be converted to a new use.

America took a particular lead in this field, for as early as 1962 an old chocolate factory in San Francisco was bought up by William M Roth, who commissioned urban designers Lawrence Halprin and Associates along with architects Bernadi and Emmons, to transform the building and grounds into shops, restaurants and a theatre. By 1979 it had blossomed into a popular leisure centre which, while preserving the atmosphere of the area, also provided much-needed jobs. This concept was then repeated in another San Francisco redevelopment, the Cannery, by Joseph Esherick Associates.

In the United Kingdom the trend really started with the renovation and redevelopment of Covent Garden (saved by local people from being knocked down to make way for a six-lane motorway) in the early 1970s. Formerly a fruit and vegetable market, it is now a popular and thriving area with numerous restaurants, shops, a market and large area for street theatre. It attracts four million tourists a year as well as indigenous Londoners, a sure sign of its success.

Similarly in Dublin in Ireland, the brewing company Guinness has converted its old hop store in the centre of the city into an art gallery and museum of brewing. Large old warehouses such as these work particularly well as exhibition spaces, with their high ceilings, long unloading doors which convert into windows, and simple uncluttered interiors.

England's 'Tate Gallery of the North' is also situated in former warehouses in Albert Dock in Liverpool. This area narrowly escaped being levelled, filled in and turned into a vast car park. Instead, in 1984 a redevelopment scheme was started and now the docks house shops, restaurants and galleries.

Similar renovation was carried out in Boston in the United States and in Bristol in Britain – where docks are in the centre of town – and to a degree in London. London's docklands, however, cover a much larger area and the development involved a great deal of new building, although in such areas as St Katherine's Dock and West India Dock an attempt was made to preserve the feel of the area by retaining some of the original buildings.

Of the old buildings which have been kept in London's docklands most are warehouses which front on to the river and have been converted into flats, that command very high prices. Old mills, made obsolete by the recession in the 1970s and changes in manufacturing techniques and demands, are also good candidates

OPPOSITE & RIGHT **Kings Cross development, Foster Associates**
The scheme involves creating offices and a park, transforming a whole area of north London.

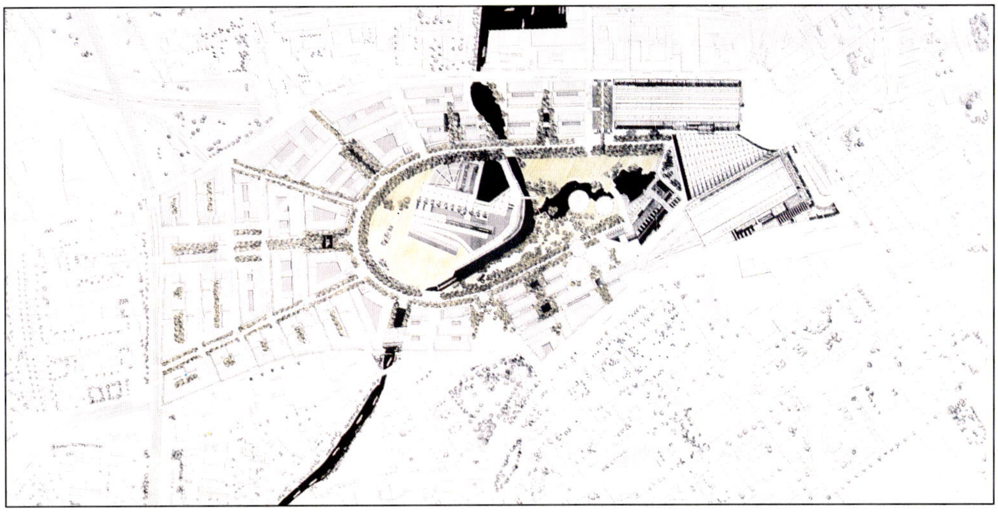

LEFT **Canary Wharf, London Docklands**
An aerial view of the site from the east shows the size of the development which will create an alternative financial centre to the City of London.

for conversion. And here the French lead the field with firms such as Reicken & Robert redeveloping and renovating many empty buildings in Elbeuf near Rouen in Normandy.

The demands of commerce and the move towards pedestrian-only areas have given rise to many interesting schemes, particularly in the United States.

The idea of streets, many covered over, devoted purely to shops and pedestrians is hardly new. In fact European cities have their old 'pedestrian precincts', for example Milan's Galleria Vittorio Emanuele II – an arcade covering two streets (designed by Giuseppe Mengoni in the mid-19th century), which contains almost 100 shops, along with restaurants and cafés. Yet with the advent of the car and the subsequent destruction wrought for its sake, many city centres became no place for strolling and browsing. Now, however, many countries are reclaiming their centres and the results, particularly in American cities, can be staggering. Two particular projects stand out – the Market Street rehabilitation scheme in San Francisco and the Angeles Plaza in Los Angeles, designed in 1983 by Dworsky Associates.

The public has learnt from the development mistakes of the 1960s and is demanding a right of veto for unsuitable plans. Where redevelopment involves a large area – such as at London's Kings Cross station – numerous models and plans have had to be submitted before any decision could be made. The Kings Cross redevelopment has, in fact, been awarded to developers Rosehaugh Stanhope which is using two sets of architects, Foster Associates and SOM.

As building costs rise and land for new development becomes more scarce – especially in cities – it is more than a commitment to conservation which encourages renovation and redevelopment, it makes good business sense – a fact which has been realized world-wide.

COMMUNITY ARCHITECTURE – THERE'S NO PLACE LIKE HOME

One morning in 1968 a woman on the 18th floor of a tower block in London struck a match to light her gas cooker and sparked off an explosion which killed her and 3 other residents, and destroyed one side of her block of flats. The disaster fuelled a controversy over housing which was to mark the end of the fashion for such alienating tower blocks and a return to smaller-scale housing.

The block was called Ronan Point, and although the unpopularity and problems caused by high-rise housing were not new when it partly collapsed, what happened that day did cause many people to re-think their views on architecture. Due to lack of money and any general public concern or awareness, governments throughout the world had been able to gloss over the problems such schemes had caused and get away with patching up defects, but once safety was seen to be at stake, governments could no longer ignore the issue, and so alternatives were seriously sought.

What grew out of this came to be known as 'community architecture' – architecture which takes into account the actual needs of people rather than requirements of ease and speed of construction. Potential users and occupants of buildings are consulted, so in effect it is architecture for the community by the community.

Besides involving the community in the concept and planning stages this idea can be taken one step further once the buildings have been finished and the residents can be involved in the running of them. This has the double advantage of maintaining the feeling of involvement and personal responsibility created during the design phase, as well as engendering pride. Also, from the government's point of view a great deal of money can be saved and pressure lifted from hard-pressed, under-staffed local authorities.

Human beings are naturally social creatures who like to group together into communities. Tower blocks which isolate them, providing them with no natural meeting places, can often create unhealthy isolation and antagonism towards the environment, leading to social problems such as vandalism. Architects had to learn that although the new flats they designed may have been far more comfortable in terms of physical needs than the slum dwellings they were replacing, they were not necessarily as comfortable as far as emotional and social needs are concerned.

In the rush to build in the 1950s and 1960s, these needs were not really top of the list of priorities for architects and planners, and huge schemes were carried out without the potential inhabitants once being canvassed for their views on the type of housing they would like.

Industrialized architecture had been exploited because of its relative cheapness and ease of erection, and in the 1960s the aim was economy of scale, with the emphasis on economy. But it soon became obvious that a house must be more than a machine for living in to be a home.

In the past, social amenities have often taken second place to factories or shops, the result being an inward-looking, frustrated community. But human beings cannot be treated as money-making commodities, they must be given the chance to be involved in their environment.

Consulting potential occupants of buildings is one way to make people feel involved – as was shown by the successful Byker development in Newcastle-upon-Tyne (1970–80), designed by Ralph Erskine, which is totally accepted by the people living in it. And rightly so, as they all had a say in its construction. The architects set up a permanent office on site and lived there during building works.

Giancarlo de Carlo used a similar approach with his Matteotti

Village in Terni, Umbria, built between 1971 and 1974 for the workers of an iron mill. He has avoided any feeling of uniformity by using 45 alternatives in the complex, which consists of a total of 250 units.

De Carlo has proved that just because a building looks similar on the outside there is no reason to make every interior identical. In Israel, Zvi Hecker has taken this idea a stage further with his futuristic Ramot Housing development on the outskirts of Jerusalem. Made up of 720 residential units (in its first phase), the primary shapes in the development are cubes and dodecahedrons, and although they are slotted together uniformly no two apartments are the same – all vary in size, shape and layout.

Besides creating feelings of individuality, another aspect of community architecture is an attempt to fit in with the environment. In the United States, schemes such as the Whitman Village Housing development on Long Island, New York (Moore Grover Harper, 1971–75) use building techniques traditional to the area – in this case wooden frames covered by shingles. This integrates the new development into the locality and so helps the residents, who are themselves local, to feel at home.

The buildings are also arranged to protect the gardens in between, which shows an understanding of how important open spaces are. And by open spaces one should not think of the bare, wind-swept no man's land surrounding so many tower blocks, but a landscaped, attractive and private area where parents will feel happy to let their children play and where people will congregate on fine days.

As the large, unwieldy and slightly brutal modern mass developments proved unpopular with inhabitants, it was natural that architects should look to vernacular architecture for ideas.

OPPOSITE **Ronan Point, London, 1968**

The collapse of a corner of the block in 1968 after a gas explosion killed four people, discredited prefabricated construction and spelt doom for many other unpopular tower blocks.

LEFT Housing authorities have learnt from their mistakes and are returning to more popular traditional styles, such as the terrace.

They might just pick superficial details such as exterior cladding which blends in with existing buildings, as in Whitman Village, or examine how buildings are grouped, how open spaces work, what sort of scale people feel comfortable with and what sort of materials they prefer? (Not surprisingly, wood and brick are very popular.) Also architects can work out how to avoid the rigid zoning so popular in the 1960s, by combining home, work and play. The result is a more humane, more thoughtful architecture which is comfortable as well as being stimulating through variety.

It is often easier for people to say what they do not like or want than to think positively but, nevertheless, architects such as Rod Hackney, Ted Cullinan and Ralph Erskine have proved that if you give people a chance to contribute towards a development they will feel happier living in it once it is completed.

OPPOSITE & RIGHT **Byker development, Newcastle-on-Tyne, Ralph Erskine, 1970–80**
This scheme broke new ground in that the future occupants were consulted every step of the way. The architects even lived on site to ensure that they were always available to the tenants.

ARCHITECT AS DESIGNER

The line between architects and more general designers is in many ways an artificial one – for after all, architects are designers of buildings, with all the added skills of understanding the technicalities of how those buildings stand up and how their various services work.

Many architects, however, have not been satisfied with restricting themselves to just creating the shell and overall look of a building, but have wanted control over the details of the interior design, right down to the furniture and fittings. And while for many modern corporate buildings the architect is expected to pick the carpets, lights and bathroom fittings and desks from a catalogue, there are those who believe, in the words of the Vienna Secessionist architect Josef Hoffmann (1870–1956), in the 'complete unity of architecture, décor and furnishings'. In fact by the mid-1980s architecture almost seemed to be taking second place to interior, furniture or product design.

At the turn of the century, architects such as Edwin Lutyens and Charles Rennie Mackintosh were designing buildings in which they kept control over every last detail – in Lutyens case even down to items such as the cost of arms he designed for the Drew family at Castle Drogo (1910–1930) in England's West Country. Movements such as Art Nouveau and Arts and Crafts attracted architects and artists alike, encouraging them to experiment with different media and in different areas – ranging from ceramics to wallpaper, and silverware to furniture.

Many contemporary architects have continued this tradition of diversification, particularly in interior design. The economic recession of the 1970s and the resulting slump in large building schemes caused many architects to look to smaller projects and many took commissions for the interiors of shops and restaurants, which they are called in to provide a definite uniqueness and individuality – which is particularly important in the constantly-changing world of retailing.

Even architects with the international stature of Norman Foster have not been able to resist the challenge and discipline of creating something completely different in a restricted space. His shop for clothes designer Katharine Hamnett on London's Brompton Road show that even world famous architects can be playful. His glass bridge from the street into the shop transforms what was once a dull, straight passage way into a magical tunnel, luring customers into the cavernous showroom beyond. Norman Foster also designed Joseph Ettedgui's British flagship shop in Sloane Street, London, Joseph however is more commonly associated with Eva Jiřićna, who designed all his other major shops. Her monochrome style, now becoming softer and more fluid, has become a much-copied trademark.

Another architect who cannot resist the challenge of shop design is Nigel Coates, of the UK NATØ group. He has applied his highly distinctive, rather anarchic style to numerous interiors, the most recent being Katharine Hamnett's newest London shop, which illustrates his fascination with 'narrative' design – the aim this time is to create the atmosphere of an early 20th-century salon.

Coates, along with such other Western architects as John Pawson and Frank Gehry, has reversed the trend of the West drawing inspiration from the East while the East remained introverted, ignoring Western talent and trends. Japan used to have no time for Western architects. Even one as celebrated as Frank Lloyd Wright received short shrift, his Imperial Hotel (1923) being torn down only 45 years after it opened – yet now Japan cannot have enough of the wild, fantasy interiors of Nigel Coates and his like.

Coates's Metropole restaurant in Tokyo (opened May 1986) was one of the first projects to truly capture the Japanese imagination, and since then his projects have included The Bohemia Jazz Club, a shop for Takeo Kikuchi and the Caffè Bongo, perhaps his best-known restaurant, and the Arc di Noe (1988). The door to the East is now open and architects such as Zaha Hadid,

OPPOSITE **Katharine Hamnett Brompton Road shop entrance, London, Norman Foster**
The glass bridge turns a dull corridor into a magical tunnel.

ABOVE **Caffè Bongo, Tokyo Nigel Coates, 1986**
One of the first foreigners to be accepted in Japan, Coates' imaginative, anarchic designs have captured the imagination of the Tokyo smart set.

LEFT **Garden seat, Edwin Lutyens**
Lutyens kept control over every last detail of his buildings – and the gardens surrounding them.

ALESSI

Richard Rogers and Aldo Rossi are all traipsing through.

Architects have long had a fascination with furniture – its look gave them a chance to practise their design skills, and its structure allowed them to draw upon their engineering knowledge. But while most architects in the early part of the century contented themselves with designing furniture to fit in whichever building they happened to be working on, it was not until Le Corbusier that architects designed furniture as an end in itself. Le Corbusier's range of modern furniture started in 1928 and, designed in collaboration with Pierre Jeanneret, his brother, and Charlotte Perriand, the pieces are firmly established as modern classics and still on sale today. His chairs were particularly successful and, in fact, chairs were also popular subjects with turn-of-the-century architects such as Richard Riemerschmid and Gaudí.

Today architects such as Frank Gehry, Zaha Hadid and Ettore Sottsass have sought to emulate these early masters with their chairs. These are chairs as works of art rather than practical objects. For example Gehry's club chair is made from cardboard – one of his favourite materials – and yet has a surprisingly solid, rounded look. Ettore Sottsass has experimented with more familiar materials – namely laminates and perspex – producing Art Deco-ish designs, while Zaha Hadid's chairs look like pieces of sculpture with their undulating curves.

While chairs and other pieces of furniture may seem like legitimate distractions for building-weary architects, product design can verge on the totally frivolous. What, one may ask, are architects doing wasting their time on items as inconsequential as candlesticks or plates? And it is quite a lot of time that is being 'wasted', in fact shops on both side of the Atlantic have sprung up to sell nothing more than architect-designed goods. Architects of the fame of Robert Venturi have designed teapots and candlesticks, and Aldo Rossi and Michael Graves are particularly active – they have both designed kettles and are now turning their attention to clocks and wrist watches. Their ultra-fashionable articles echo the objectives of the Werkbund, founded 80 years earlier.

Architects are ceasing to treat their profession as a narrow specialization and are moving towards the wider design field, in the manner of early 20th-century masters, and it seems that nothing is too small to merit the attention of the world's leading architects. After all a commission is a commission, whether it be for a clock or a cathedral.

Assorted designer goods from Alessi. Clockwise from top, a Robert Venturi cuckoo clock, an Aldo Rossi kettle and Michael Graves' mantel clock. Even world-famous architects are allowed to be frivolous.

GLOSSARY

BAUHAUS
German design school with Arts & Crafts roots founded in Weimar in 1906 and reorganized in 1919 under Walter Gropius, who renamed it Bauhaus; the word has come to epitomize the design philosophy of the 1925-32 period of the Dessau Bauhaus. In architecture and design today, 'Bauhaus' connotes austere Functionalism, the use of industrial materials, concrete, glass and stainless steel, the absence of ornament and, typically, flat roofs.

BRUTALISM
Architectural style that, in a heavy-handed pursuit of tight budgeting and unsparing Functionalism, seems to trample on the public's sensitivities. In reality, it was some 1950s and 1960s architects' preference for raw concrete surfaces and harsh technical solutions to problems which first inspired the 'Brutalist' tag.

BUILDING SERVICES
Mostly internal ie, hidden, systems necessary to make a building work and keep it safe and comfortable; principally electricity, water and sewage, including sprinklers, telecommunication and computer networking cables, lifts and escalators, air-conditioning and central heating.

CIAM
Les Congrès Internationaux d'Architecture Moderne, the largely Le Corbusier-inspired wing of the Modern Movement's intellectual élite. From 1928 until soon after the end of World War II, CIAM served both as a symbol of progressive architecture and town planning, and as a forum for the international exchange of ideas.

CLADDING, SEE CURTAIN WALL

CONSTRUCTIVISM
Russian art movement which emerged after the 1917 revolution. For inspiration, Constructivists looked to industrial methods and materials, and were interested in the dynamic, often abstract, aspects of composition and design. Leading figures included Kasimir Malevich, Vladimir Tatlin and El Lissitzky.

CURTAIN WALL
Thin, light outer membrane on a large, rigid-framed structure replacing walls with windows. Usually a cladding of glass and light metals, keeping out the wet and cold and normally letting in far more light than windows.

DADA(ISM)
Literary and artistic movement of the early 20th century determined to reject everything normally considered 'art'. Nurtured in Switzerland between 1914 and 1919 by cosmopolitan émigrés, Tristan Tzara, Hans Arp et al, 'dada' was meant to be a babyspeak shout in defiance of the social and artistic establishment. Its influence on young architects of the 1920s was more sympathetic than direct.

DE STIJL
Dutch magazine meaning 'The Style', espousing abstraction and the unity of the arts, as well as the artists, designers and architects supporting its philosophy, the latter group forming a bridge between pre-World War I Expressionists and 1920s Modernists. Above all, the application of fresh ideas to community-housing projects by De Stijl designers announced the social dimension of architecture for this century.

DECONSTRUCTIVISM
Term in the fast-expanding vocabulary of Post-Modernism, covering the aims of some, mainly American, architects who want to feel free from all formal preconceptions about building, while sometimes using sophisticated engineering techniques to achieve their aims.

DOUBLE VERTEBRATE
Twin-'spines' feature of Milan's Pirelli building, 1959; designed by Gio Ponti, Pier-Luigi Nervi et al, each containing a separate core as a duct for the building services.

DYMAXION
R Buckminster Fuller's label for innovative projects in which he applied scientific thinking and new technology to design problems, eg, 'Dymaxion House', 1929, a glass and metal domestic environment, suspended from a central service stalk, and 'Dymaxion Transport Unit' (early 1930s), a rear-engined, three-wheel aerodynamic automobile.

EXPRESSIONISM
Primarily an art movement associated with Germany, Austria and Switzerland, but also a kind of architecture in those same countries. The Expressionist architect attempted to express an inner vision, eg, Hermann Finsterlin, who was unfettered by engineering or structural restraints. In fact, Expressionist architecture is documented more richly in project drawings than in completed buildings.

FENESTRATION
The arrangement of windows.

FUNCTIONALISM
Probably the single most important tenet of Modern Movement architects and designers, who asserted that nothing should be introduced into any design that does not perform a function, no ornament for its own sake, and that nothing should be made or built that does not have a proper function.

GABLE
The triangular wall closing the end of a pitched roof.

GARDEN CITY
A British movement, put forth by Ebenezer Howard in 1898, which attempted to rationalize town and country planning. The aim was to house whole populations in semirural settlements, but the model was already out of date soon after the first Garden Cities (Letchworth, 1903, Welwyn, 1920), were started.

GEODESIC DOME
A large spherical building or hemispherical dome comprising conjoined polygonal units which support each other all around to form a shell strong enough to carry interior floors and services. Used in rapidly built industrial spaces, and as spectacular exhibition buildings, eg at Expo '67 in Montreal.

HEIMATSTIL, DER
The version of Vernacular architecture favoured for housing in Hitler's Germany. With roots in Central Europe, it emphasized rural themes — among them, pitched roofs, round coaching arches and flower boxes.

HISTORICISM
Architecture based on the belief that the design language of an earlier period can be reused in the present. Often leads to sympathetic recreations of buildings of the past, although its huge success in the Victorian age markedly waned in the 20th century.

INDUSTRIALIZED BUILDING
Factory-made building components, beams, slabs, window frames, etc; offer a better-controlled, more economical process than on-site construction. See also System Building.

LOAD-BEARING

Building elements which help to distribute the load ie, the weight of the materials it is made of, through the structure to the foundations. In pre-industrial building, the load was mainly carried by thick external walls and massive piers, but with the use of steel frames and reinforced concrete, it became possible to construct much smaller load-bearing units capable of holding up heavier and taller buildings.

NEO-VERNACULAR

A strand of Post-Modernism marked by a deliberate return to traditional, particularly local, models. By bringing back the detailing, but seldom the construction methods, of a century or more ago, some Post-Modern architects appeal to a public put off by the impersonal feeling of much Modernist-inspired building.

NEUE SACHLICHKEIT, DIE

German term meaning 'a new matter-of-factness' describing the change of mood among avant-garde designers around the time of World War I, away from the self-indulgent extravagances of Expressionist architecture towards more practical and socially useful work. The term is sometimes called 'New Objectivity' in English.

NEW OBJECTIVITY, SEE NEUE SACHLICHKEIT

PARABOLIC ARCH

An arch formed from the 'thinner' end of the geometric figure of a parabola, largely made possible by the introduction of reinforced concrete.

PILOTIS

The load-bearing piles left free-standing and exposed in an open-ground-floor space, making it look like a house on stilts. Often wider at the top than bottom, *pilotis* (a French word meaning 'pile-driven foundation raft') became a kind of trademark of Le Corbusier's designs from the 1920s until c1950. Their original aim was to provide parking and play space below a housing block, but this was outweighed by the heat loss due to lack of ground insulation.

PLURALISM

Unabashed borrowing of at times wildly incongruous design and other elements by contemporary architects.

POST-MODERNISM

The broadly used label for recent developments in architecture that have broken with the functional ideals of the Modern Movement. Shows an anti-purist delight in shapes for their own sake and in plundering any historicist style for motifs. Traditional materials like brick and timber are favoured for exteriors, but up-to-date construction methods are not shunned. Mainstream Post-Modern architecture of the past two decades often features patterned brickwork, pitched roofs, turrets and round windows.

PRE-STRESSED CONCRETE

Extra-strong beams pre-cast in a factory and included in a reinforced concrete frame that is built on site. To make pre-stressed beams, high-strength steel wires are stretched the length of a moulding box before the mix is poured in. When set, the wires are released and the tension pulls the ends of the beam towards the middle.

PREFAB

Popular name for factory-made units assembled as emergency housing for bombed-out British citizens in the last years of World War II and the immediate postwar reconstruction period. Although the 'prefabricated' bungalows were not designed to last, the experience of making them prepared the way for later techniques of system building.

REINFORCED CONCRETE

Type of concrete obtained from pouring the mix into a mould (formwork) containing rolled steel bars, wires or mesh, or around a steel girder, giving it greater strength when set. Can be done on site or in a factory. A further advance on this technique is pre-stressed concrete.

RENDERED/UNRENDERED

A term meaning that a wall of brick, masonry or concrete is either with or without a coating of cement, plaster etc.

TENSION OR TENSILE STRUCTURES, SEE *SPACE FRAMES*

WALKWAYS

High-level communication passages and bridges linking blocks of flats or recreational buildings. Highly favoured by Le Corbusier for his Mediterranean projects, but largely unsuitable in damp and windy Britain, where it was detested by residents.

RIBBON WINDOWS

A continuous glazed opening the length of a building floor, an innovation made possible by the use of steel or reinforced concrete frames. Particularly suitable for lighting office blocks and department stores.

SECESSION, VIENNA (Wiener Sezession)

Group of radical Viennese artists who in 1897 opened their own rival exhibition in defiance of the academic establishment. Mainly painters, they warmly welcomed new-wave trends from all over Europe. One of the founding members, Josef Olbrich, designed their hall in 1898-99.

SHUTTER(ED)

Used in combination with the word 'concrete', shuttering describes the impressions left by the wooden panels, or shutters, of the formwork — the moulds into which the wet concrete is poured. Some architects like the authentic look of a material that declares openly, when set, how it has been formed, while others play with the effects of grained timber that are often printed on the surface of the concrete by the rough inner surfaces of the planks.

SPACE FRAMES

Describes a wide variety of structures, all having in common the manipulation of skins, or membranes, cables and posts to cover or enclose spaces. Tension and elasticity are the principles chiefly involved, and architects can call on new high-tech materials made of plastics and alloys to help them design larger and stronger 'tent houses'.

STREAMLINING

The fast-developing science of aerodynamics for aviation and racing cars in the early 1920s which provided images for technological design eagerly taken up by Modernist architects. Although mostly purposeless in terms of structural dynamics, airflow forms were adopted into the design vocabulary of concrete architecture.

STRESSED SKIN STRUCTURES, SEE *SPACE FRAMES*

SYSTEM BUILDING

The application of the 'Lego' or 'Meccano' principle of standardized components in industrialized building methods. Ambitious programmes of school building and housing can be speeded up by using mass-produced components, but the resulting sameness has made system building unpopular; for factories, however, the low costs make it acceptable.

INDEX

Page numbers in *italics* refer to relevant captions.

ACKNOWLEDGEMENTS

The authors and publishers have made every endeavour to identify the copyright owners of the photographs used in this publication; they apologize for any omissions and would like to thank the following:

Key: *t* = top; *b* = bottom; *l* = left; *r* = right

Alessi: page 122. Architectural Association: pages 7 *t b*, 12*tr*, 30/31, 31 *b*, 33, 38, 40 *b*, 41 *t*, 43, 46 *t b*, 47, 50, 50/51, 51 *r*, 52, 54 *b*, 54/55, 58 *r*, 66 *b*, 68 *tl*, 90 *t b*, 95 *t*, 102, 103, 105 *t*, 108, 118, 119, 121 *t*. Austrian National Tourist Office: page 18 *b*. Barbican Centre/photo Peter Bloomfield: pages 70, 84. Dave Burton: page 108/109. Olympia & York: pages 94/95, 115 *b*. City of Bristol: page 112 *l*. Liz Eddison: pages 31 *t*, 56 *t*, 57, 61 *t*, 62 *t*, 121 *b*. Nick Eddison: page 15. Norman Foster & Associates: pages 6, 92, 99 *l r b*, 114, 115 *t*, 120. French Government Tourist Office: page 111 *b*. Phil Green: page 96 *b*. Guinness: pages 112/113, 113. Angelo Hornak: pages 8, 12 *br*, 19, 20, 25 *t*, 39, 49, 60, 61 *b*, 62 *b*, 64, 67, 78/79, 81, 87, 89, 101, 110, 111 *t*, 117. A F Kersting: pages 17, 27, 29, 77 *t*. Lever Brothers Company: page 80 *l*. University of Leicester: page 86. Creative Company/Milton Keynes Development Corporation: page 78 *b*. Museum of Finnish Architecture: page 56 *b*. Robert Opie: page 63. Portmeiron: page 105 *b*. Polly Powell: pages 16, 36, 65 *l r*, 73, 76, 109. Royal Institute of British Architects (RIBA): pages 21 *b*, 28, 32 *l r*, 34 *t b*, 35, 45, 53, 66 *t*, 68 *tr b*, 74 *b*, 77 *b*, 80 *r*, 83. Richard Rogers Partnership Ltd: pages 96 *t*, 97 *t b*, 98. South Bank Centre: page 85. Spanish National Tourist Office: pages 10, 14. Ed Teitelman: pages 11, 13, 18 *t*, 21 *t*, 22, 22/23, 23, 24, 25 *b*, 28/29, 41 *b*, 42/43, 44, 48 *t b*, 58 *l*, 58/59, 59 *r*, 69, 72, 75, 82 *l r*, 91, 100 *t b*, 106, 107 *t b*. Alan Williams: page 104.

BIBLIOGRAPHY

ALLEN, Gerald, *Charles Moore*, Watson-Gupthill Publications Inc, New York, 1980.
ALLSOPP, Bruce, *Towards a More Humane Architecture*, Frederick Muller, London, 1974
BANHAM, Reyner, *Design by Choice*, Academu Editions, London 1981
BARFORD, George, *Understanding Modern Architecture*, Davis Publications, 1986
CURTIS, William J R, *Modern Architecture Since 1900*, Phaidon Press Ltd, Oxford, 1982
DE WITT, Denis & DE WITT, Elizabeth, *Modern Architecture in Europe – A Guide to Buildings Since the Industrial Revolution*, Weidenfeld & Nicholson Ltd, London, 1987
DREXLER, Arthur, *Transformations in Modern Architecture*, Secker & Warburg Ltd, London, 1980
GIBBERD, Vernon, *Architecture Source Book*, Macdonald Orbis, London, 1988; Wellfleet Press, Secaucus, NJ, 1988
HOLLINGSWORTH, Mary, *Architecture – The 20th Century*, Brompton Books, London, 1988
JENCKS, Charles, *The Language of Post-Modern Architecture*, Academy Editions, London, 1987
JENCKS, Charles, *Late-Modern Architecture*, Academy Editions, 1980
JENCKS, Charles, *Modern Movements in Architecture*, Penguin Books Ltd, Middx, 1973
JENCKS, Charles (ed), *Post-Modern Classicism*, Academy Editions, London, 1980
JOHNSON, Philip & WIGLEY, Mark, *Deconstructivist Architecture*, MOMA, New York, 1988
KAPLAN, Sam Hall, *LA Lost and Found*, Viking, London, 1987
KNEVITT, Charles, *Space on Earth*, Thames-Methuen, London, 1985
KOSTOFF, Spiro, *A History of Architecture*, Oxford University Press, Oxford, 1985
KULTERMANN, Udo, *Architecture in the Seventies*, The Architectural Press Ltd, London, 1980
LAMPUGNANI, V M, *Architecture and City Planning in the 20th Century*, Van Nostrand Reinhold Co Ltd, London 1980
LAMPUGNANI, VM, *Encyclopaedia of 20th-Century Architecture*, Thames & Hudson Ltd, London, 1963
LAWRENCE, Roderick J, *Housing, Dwellings and Homes*, John Wiley & Sons Ltd, Chichester, 1987
NUTTGENS, Patrick, *Understanding Modern Architecture*, Unwin Hyman, 1988
PEVSNER, Nikolaus, *Sources of Modern Architecture and Design*, Thames & Hudson Ltd, London , 1968
RUSSELL, Frank (ed), *Art Nouveau Architecture*, Academy Editions, London, 1979
SHARP, Denis, *Modern Architecture and Expressionism*, Longmans Greer & Co, London, 1966
SUDJIC, Deyan, *New Directions in British Architecture: Norman Foster, Richard Rogers, James Stirling*, Thames & Hudson Ltd, London, 1986
TAFURI, Manfredo & Dal CO, Francesco, *Modern Architecture*, Barrie & Jenkins, London, 1986
WHITFORD, Frank, *Bauhaus*, Thames & Hudson Ltd, London, 1984